SAFE AT ALL TIMES

SAFE AT ALL TIMES

Protecting Yourself and Your Family in a Dangerous World

Detective Janet Rodgers

THE READER'S DIGEST ASSOCIATION, INC.

Pleasantville, New York/Montreal

For all of the courageous survivors out there and for those
who want to take control of their own lives—**stay safe.**

A READER'S DIGEST BOOK

This edition published by The Reader's Digest Association
by arrangement with Carroll & Brown Limited

Copyright © 2002

Conceived and produced by

CARROLL & BROWN PUBLISHERS LIMITED

20 Lonsdale Road, Queen's Park, London, NW6 6RD

Text copyright © 2002 Janet Rodgers

Illustrations and compilation copyright © 2002 Carroll & Brown Limited

FOR CARROLL & BROWN LIMITED

Project Editor	**Kirsten Chapman**
Managing Editors	**Becky Alexander**
	and Michelle Bernard
Designer	**Roland Codd**
Photography	**Jules Selmes**

FOR READER'S DIGEST

U.S. Project Editors	**Susan Byrne, Nanette Bendyna**
Canadian Project Editor	**Pamela Johnson**
Project Designer	**George McKeon**
Executive Editor, Trade Publishing	**Dolores York**
Senior Design Director	**Elizabeth Tunnicliffe**
Editorial Director	**Christopher Cavanaugh**
Director, Trade Publishing	**Christopher T. Reggio**
Vice President & Publisher, Trade Publishing	**Harold Clarke**

Library of Congress Cataloging-in-Publication Data

Rodgers, Janet, 1960-
Safe at all times: protecting yourself and your family in a dangerous world / Janet Rodgers.
p. cm.
Includes index
ISBN 0-7621-0398-1
1. Crime prevention. 2. Safety education. 3. Self-defense. I. Title.

HV7431 .R59 2002
362.88--dc21
2002068109

NOTE TO OUR READERS

This publication contains the opinions and ideas of its author and is designed to provide useful information
to the reader on the subject matter covered. No self-defense measures are without risk. Before engaging in any actions
that may be suggested in or relate to the subject of this publication, always consider the circumstances carefully and use your
best judgment. This publication is sold with the understanding that the author and the publisher are not engaged in rendering
advice. Laws vary from one jurisdiction to another, and readers with specific issues should seek the services of an attorney.
The publisher and the author specifically disclaim any responsibility for any liability, loss or risk (personal, financial,
or otherwise), which may be claimed or incurred as a consequence, directly or indirectly, of the use and/or
application of any of the contents of this publication.

The terms "he" and "she" should be read as interchangeable in this book and are in no way intended
as representative of the genders of criminals or victims.

Address any comments about *Safe at All Times* to:
The Reader's Digest Association, Inc.
Adult Trade Publishing
Reader's Digest Road
Pleasantville, NY 10570-7000

For more Reader's Digest products and information, visit our Web site:
www.rd.com (in the United States)
www.readersdigest.ca (in Canada)

Reproduced by Colourscan in Singapore
Printed by Canale in Italy

1 3 5 7 9 10 8 6 4 2

CONTENTS

"What we can do is arm ourselves with the information to keep ourselves and our families as safe as possible."

FOREWORD

On July 27, 1981, my 6-year-old son Adam was abducted and later found murdered. My life was forever changed. I vowed that Adam's death would not be in vain, and I have spent my days since then fighting for victims' rights—and for the last 15 years, taking that fight to the airwaves as host of the Fox television program *America's Most Wanted*.

In speaking with victims and families over the years, I often hear the words "if only..." It is the refrain that haunts the family of anyone who has been a victim of crime: "If only I had done this or that, then maybe things would be different today." I try to offer comfort and solace to the victims of crime and to their families. Do not torture yourselves, I try to advise: It is not your fault. We can't protect ourselves from every danger.

What we can do is arm ourselves with the information to keep ourselves and our families as safe as possible. And *Safe at All Times* does that.

I have found in these pages the kind of practical, sensible advice that so many people seek: ways to become more aware, to stay more prepared, to have the confidence to take control of your surroundings, and to know how to react in a dangerous situation.

I always tell families, you can't live your life in fear. You can't jump at every shadow. And you can't make your kids terrified of the world. But knowledge is power, and you can talk about ways of becoming more street smart—and make learning about safety a real part of your daily life.

I hope you will read *Safe at All Times*, but more important, I hope you will use the information you find inside—and share it with your family and friends.

Never has the need for public safety and personal protection been so great. I applaud Reader's Digest for making *Safe at All Times* an accessible, comprehensive handbook, giving each of us more power to shift the balance of safety to our favor.

John Walsh
America's Most Wanted

A NOTE FROM THE AUTHOR

Nobody likes to think about the possibility of being attacked or robbed. But unfortunately, these risks to our personal safety are a reality of everyday life. As a veteran member of London's Metropolitan Police Service, I have discovered that self-defense and awareness lessons can help everyone—men, women, children, and older people alike—stay safe.

Safe at All Times is the secret weapon each of us can use to take positive action. Using simple, easy-to-learn techniques, this book will guide you on how best to avoid dangerous situations and guard against physical attack. Among the chapters, you'll find: how to use common items such as umbrellas and pens as weapons; how to make your home and workplace as safe as possible; what to do in the worst cases of street mugging, road rage, and plane hijacking; and how to ensure the safety of children, teens, and older people. If you have always intended to do something about improving your security but have never gotten around to it, this is just the resource you need to get started.

By reading this book, you will gain self-confidence and knowledge you can share with friends and family. Then you can make the world a safer place in which to live. Your well-being and that of your loved ones depend on it.

Detective Janet Rodgers

1

stay **aware**, stay **safe**

Major disasters can cause us to fear for our safety, but just what are the risks that we need to protect against? Prepare yourself mentally for dealing with emergencies, and do something practical by assembling a disaster supply kit for your home. Plus, discover ways to help others without jeopardizing your personal safety.

how safe are you?

The cataclysmic events of the last several years, including the terrorist jet bombings in New York City on September 11, 2001, the Columbine High School massacre in Colorado, and the Oklahoma City federal building bombing, have caused many of us to fear for our lives and those of our families. However, part of the process of moving on from these disasters involves positive action. On one level the tragedies raise questions for the authorities and lead to reviews of public safety. These events also cause us to think of ways we can protect ourselves and stay safe at all times.

Statistically, we are most at risk during everyday activities, such as going to work; relatively few of us encounter terrorist activities or serious criminals.

It's important to bear in mind that these events are not normal; they dominate the news because they are sensational. We all know deep down—but don't always remember—that what we encounter in our everyday lives can be far more threatening than the actions of terrorists or criminals. In the United States, more than 40,000 people die in motor vehicle accidents every year, compared to 120 who die in airline crashes. And an average of 430,000 people die from smoking-related illnesses, compared to the five deaths attributed to anthrax poisonings in 2001—and those were the first anthrax-related deaths in two decades. Learning to protect ourselves from large-scale events is important, but so is examining our everyday safety habits.

what are the risks?

When considering risks to our well-being, a look at the 10 leading causes of death in the United States can put things into perspective. After age 34, cancer and heart disease are the most common causes of death; below that age, accidents are by far the highest killers. To beat the odds of developing cancer or heart disease, we can attempt to lead healthy lives with a good diet and plenty of exercise. Avoiding accidents often takes simple common sense, but we also can improve safety with preparation and good practice, such as child-proofing our homes (see page 132) and driving defensively (see page 48).

Despite the statistics, however, crime is a major fear, largely because we feel that we have little control over it—others do it to us and it's often unexpected. But awareness can help us stay safe. This is why much of this book is dedicated to avoiding and dealing with crime.

violent crime decreasing

Although you can never predict the situation that you might find yourself in, it can help to look at the general crime trends and specific crime characteristics. Despite people's fears, the good news is that there has been a marked decline in crime rates in recent years. According to the latest Federal Bureau of Investigation's Uniform Crime Reports, the crime index—the rate of violent crimes in the United States—fell for the ninth consecutive year in 2000. The National Crime Victimization Survey (NCVS) of 2000—the other major indicator of U.S. crime rates—showed similar findings: Robbery and assault rates have declined steadily since 1994, and homicide rates have dropped to levels last seen in 1967.

In Canada, the story is similar. Figures from Statistics Canada show that from 1999 to 2000,

violent and property crime (burglary and theft) decreased by 2.4 percent—a trend that continued from the previous eight years. The rate of homicides was three times lower in Canada than in the United States.

factors affecting crime

Overall crime rates hint at the state of the nation but don't necessarily relate to how crime affects individuals. The NCVS says the following factors can influence whether you're likely to become a victim:

- **GENDER** In general, men are victims of violent crime more often than women and, according to the FBI's Uniform Crime Reports, three-quarters of murder victims in 1999 were male. Men are also more likely to be the victims of carjackings. The exception to this trend is rape and sexual assault. Also, women are more likely to be victimized by somebody that they know.
- **AGE** Younger people are more likely than older people to suffer property and violent crime, but of the crimes committed against people age 65 and older, the rate of property crime is disproportionately high, accounting for more than nine in 10 offenses.
- **LEVEL OF INCOME** The higher the household income, the lower the chance of becoming a victim of violent crime. Low-income households are more likely to experience burglary (breaking and entering), while high-income households are more likely to experience property and auto theft.
- **WHERE YOU LIVE** Violent crime rates are highest among urban residents, followed by suburban residents. Rural areas experience the lowest rates of violent crime. Property crime is far more likely to happen to renters than to homeowners.

planning for problems

Crime, terrorist activities, and disasters create fear because they seem so random and unpredictable. You can't control everything, but you can take the time to think about what you would do in an emergency. If you do your research, you can minimize the dangers and cope with the aftermath.

improve your awareness

When going about your daily activities, it's easy to forget about everyday risks. At work, you may get used to stepping over loose wires near your desk; on the street, you answer your cell phone when it rings; and in the supermarket parking lot, you concentrate your attention on loading your car with groceries. You're probably not thinking about tripping on a wire, having your phone stolen, or getting mugged. However, in order to protect yourself effectively, you have to be better aware of your surroundings.

analyze your routine

Over the course of the next few days, try to assess all the risks of everything you do: As you are driving, look for danger spots and consider how your driving might affect others (see page 48); if you travel alone at night, do you stay in well-lighted areas, and do you know places you could go for help (see page 33)? Around the house, what might cause you to trip or knock something over (see page 161)? If you are doing anything that might be putting you at risk, be prepared to make changes.

Are you putting yourself at risk? Making a call on the street can distract you from possible dangers. Instead, do it when you're inside a safe place.

read the danger signals

Sensing, processing, and evaluating the world around us is something we do without thinking. When having a conversation, for example, you pick up on small changes in a person's tone of voice or facial expression and are able to recognize if he is becoming angry or threatening even before he says anything specific. Whether you call this a "gut reaction," "intuition," or "natural instincts," this is what helps us avoid or react to danger and, ultimately, to survive.

Sometimes acting on these signals might go against your social conditioning. For example, if you are in an office and a work colleague suddenly becomes crude, suggestive, or abusive, you might get embarrassed and hesitate to say or do anything for fear of causing a scene. But your primary objective should always be to protect yourself. Trust your instincts and act upon them. Tell the colleague directly that you object to the way he is talking to you. If his offensive behavior continues, be prepared to take the matter further (see page 46).

prepare for fear

In dangerous situations, fear can cause some profound physical reactions, for which you should be ready. In moments of crisis, some people freeze and have difficulty talking or screaming. Some become disoriented and have trouble understanding what is going on. In extreme situations, some people vomit, defecate, or urinate—all of which are involuntary and should not be read as a sign of weakness. Another major physical response is the body's release of the hormone adrenaline, which is called the "fight or flight" syndrome. This is the most useful aspect of fear (see box, right).

choose a course of action

Although most of us no longer have to use our survival instincts, we do still have them. Bear this in mind if you're worried that you wouldn't know what to do if you were attacked, had an accident, or were in a disaster. Nobody can tell you the perfect course of action, as each situation is different, but, basically, if confronted with an emergency you should take the following steps:

- **ASSESS THE SITUATION** Working quickly and using all your senses, establish exactly what

WHAT HAPPENS WHEN...

ADRENALINE IS RELEASED

The adrenaline "rush" is probably the most useful aspect of fear because it enables you to take evasive action. Adrenaline causes your heart and breathing rates to increase, meaning more oxygen can reach your brain and muscles. These processes, in turn, mean that your senses become more acute and your brain works faster. You will feel lighter on your feet and stronger than normal.

Adrenaline also numbs pain for a short time, and many people who are hurt in fights report that they don't feel the pain of injuries until they have calmed down. Because of these physical changes, an adrenaline rush can help you defend yourself (see page 68), especially if you have practiced the self-defense techniques in this book.

has happened and whether there are any continuing risks to yourself or others.

- **MAKE IT SAFE** If there are any remaining hazards, you may need to remove them before doing anything else. For example, following a car accident, one of the first things you should do is switch off the ignition, even if the engine isn't running. Or if there is an earthquake, turning off the utilities at the main switches can prevent fires, floods, or explosions (see page 17).

- **GET HELP** In most emergency situations you will require help, whether it's from emergency services or from passersby. If you are being attacked in the street, screaming may scare off your assailant and bring people to your aid (see page 72).

- **USE FIRST AID** If someone is seriously injured, you may need to give emergency treatment, such as cardiopulmonary resuscitation (CPR).

Finally, trust yourself to make the right decision. It will be based on your instinctive assessment of the facts at hand, as well as your common sense, your previous experience, and the advice in books such as this.

emergency planning

You might wonder how anyone can be ready for every emergency because fires, floods, and manmade disasters all have such different effects. However, the preparations you make for one type of event are probably very similar to those you might need in another. The following advice is based on the "Family Disaster Plan" developed by the U.S. Federal Emergency Management Agency, the American Red Cross, and the Canadian Red Cross. For information on creating an emergency supplies kit, see page 20.

Assemble an evacuation kit. If you have to leave your home because of a major disaster, you won't have time to think about what to include. Plan what to take now, and keep it in a large bag or trunk near your front door.

research the risks

Before you can effectively prepare for disasters, you need to find out what type you might face in your area. Your local Red Cross or emergency management office will be able to assist you (see page 170). Request information on preparing for specific disasters, such as floods, earthquakes, or tornadoes, and learn the emergency plans at your workplace, your children's school or day care center, or other places where you or your family spend time. If there are shelters, do you know where they are? Ask if there are any community warning signals in place, how to tell what each one means, and what to do if you hear them. Bear in mind that some warnings may be communicated by radio or television.

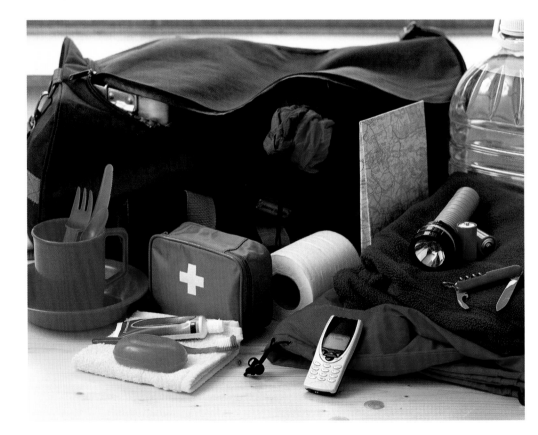

devise a plan

Take time to discuss with your family the disasters that may happen and the importance of sticking to a plan. One of the most important things to consider is a point of contact. Ask an out-of-town friend or relative to act as contact person for phone calls because it's often easier to phone long distance than locally in disaster situations. Make sure that everyone in the family knows the phone number of this person or keeps it with them at all times.

Note all your family members' e-mail addresses, as well as that of your out-of-town contact person; if the phone lines are busy following a disaster, e-mails may still get through.

Also, establish two meeting points. One location should be close to your home—perhaps a tree in your street or a neighbor's house—where you can meet in case of a sudden emergency, such as a fire. The other location should be outside your neighborhood, perhaps at or near an emergency shelter in the area or somewhere farther away, such as at the home of a relative in another town or state. However, bear in mind that, in many circumstances, it is safest for everyone to follow the evacuation procedures of your office or school. Type up your communication plan and meeting points and display a copy in a prominent place in your home. Also, consider the preparations you can make in your home (see box, right).

Once you have put all of your safety measures in place, don't get complacent. Remind everyone of the plans and practice home evacuations every six months. Keep all of your records and phone numbers up to date, and don't forget to restock food and water supplies in emergency kits (see page 20).

DISASTER-PROOF YOUR HOME

In case of emergencies, protect your property and make your home safe with these measures:

☐ **Assemble a supply kit** See page 20 for the items you should include. It will be useful in all sorts of disasters.

☐ **Check your insurance** Make sure that your house is covered for the type of disasters that occur in your area. Insurance against earthquakes or floods is often not included in standard policies, and you may need to buy an additional policy.

☐ **Consider your pets** Animals aren't allowed in emergency shelters, so ask out-of-town friends or a nearby animal shelter if they will take your pets if you have to evacuate your home.

☐ **Establish escape routes** Find two escape routes from every room in your home. Make sure that everyone knows these.

☐ **Find safe places** In case of hurricanes, floods, or other disasters, some parts of your home will be safer than others. Determine where those are for each possible situation and make sure that everyone knows them. In some cases you may need to evacuate. For procedures visit the Web site of the Red Cross (www.redcross.org in the United States and www.redcross.ca in Canada).

☐ **Learn how to switch off your utilities** In many disasters, such as an earthquake, the danger doesn't end with the event. Floods, fires, and explosions can be caused by leaks, so make sure everyone knows how to turn off the gas, water, and electricity at the main switches.

☐ **List emergency telephone numbers** Note the numbers for the fire department, police, ambulance, electric and gas companies, doctor, dentist, pharmacy, taxi, and veterinarian, and make sure a list is kept by all the phones in the home. Also include everyone's work and school numbers and e-mail addresses, and those of your emergency out-of-town contact.

Install smoke alarms (right) on the ceiling or high on a wall. On stairways, position the alarm in the path of smoke moving up the stairs.

Purchase a fire extinguisher (center) and fire blanket. Check that everyone in the family knows how to use them—get training from your local fire department if necessary.

If you are trapped (far right), force towels or sheets into the cracks of the door to help prevent smoke from creeping in. Or seal the cracks with duct tape or something similar.

protect yourself against fire

The U.S. Department of Health and Human Services estimates that, in 2000, house fires accounted for more than $5 million in property damage and claimed the lives of a civilian every two and a half hours. In Canada, fires are the third leading cause of accidental death, according to the Canada Safety Council. Being prepared for fires can make the difference between life and death.

The most effective prevention against a fire in your home is to install smoke alarms.

Smoke alarms cut the chances of dying in a house fire by 40 to 50 percent, according to the U.S. Department of Health and Human Services.

Smoke alarms are cheap and easy to install and maintain. Make sure that you have one on every level of your home and outside sleeping areas, and check that everyone can hear them from where they sleep. It is possible to get alarms that flash for the hearing impaired. Don't put smoke alarms in kitchens, bathrooms, or garages, as the steam, smoke, or fumes in these areas might set off false alarms. Once a month, dust the alarms and test them using the test buttons. If your alarm doesn't work, get a new one. Change the batteries at least once a year.

Teach your children what to do if there is a fire in the home and practice your drill regularly. Then follow this advice from the U.S. National Fire Protection Association (www.nfpa.org):

- **CRAWL LOW** Some of the smoke and toxic gases produced by a fire will rise to the ceiling while other fumes will sink. You can find the best air by crawling with your head at 1 to 2 ft. (30 to 60 cm) above the floor. Close doors behind you as you go.
- **CHECK DOORS** If a door is closed, feel the door and the doorknob before you open it. If they're cool and there is no smoke seeping through the cracks, it should be safe to open.
- **USE ALTERNATIVE ESCAPE ROUTES** If one route from a room is blocked, then use another.

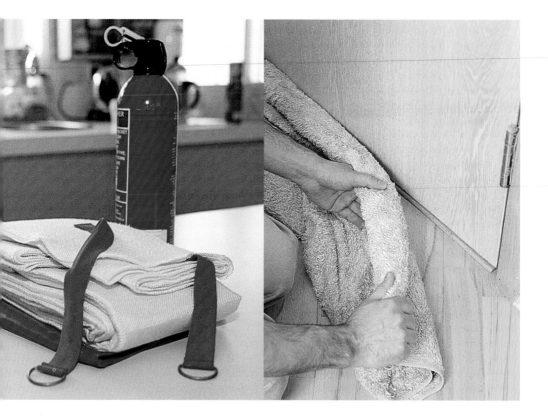

If you are trapped in an upstairs room, be prepared to jump. Throw mattresses or clothing out the window to help break your fall. Don't jump straight out. Lower yourself by your hands, hang, and then drop.

- **GET HELP IF TRAPPED** If you can't get out of a room, for example, because it's too high up to jump, wedge towels and sheets under the closed door to stop smoke from getting in. Open the window for ventilation. Attract the attention of neighbors and firefighters by shouting for help, hanging a sheet out the window, or, if there is a phone in the room, by calling the emergency services.

- **GET OUTSIDE QUICKLY** Don't stop to call the fire department from inside the home, as you may be overcome by smoke and toxic fumes. Get out quickly and then call for help. Warn your neighbors, as they may be in danger. Never go back inside to rescue possessions, pets, or others.

- **STOP, DROP, AND ROLL** If your clothes or body are on fire, don't run around, but drop to the ground, cover your face, and roll around to put out the fire. Practice this with your kids so that it becomes an instinctive reaction.

install carbon monoxide detectors

Another essential in every home is a carbon monoxide detector. According to the Canada Safety Council, carbon monoxide is the leading cause of fatal poisonings in North America. This gas may get into your home through a faulty furnace, range, water heater, or fireplace. It is particularly dangerous because it is colorless, tasteless, and odorless.

Protect yourself by installing carbon monoxide detectors on each level of your home. If the alarm on your detector is triggered, turn off all appliances and sources of combustion and open doors and windows. Call a technician to fix the faulty appliance. If anyone is showing symptoms that are similar to the flu, including headache, fatigue, nausea, and difficulty breathing, immediately get everyone out into the fresh air and call the fire department.

six disaster basics

Disaster can strike quickly and often without warning. It is essential to be prepared for emergencies that might affect your home, such as a gas leak, flood, or hurricane. You can protect yourself from some disasters by fitting devices such as smoke alarms or a carbon monoxide detector (see page 19). However, in the event of a large-scale disaster, the whole area may be affected, so you will need to have an emergency supply kit to provide you and your family with basic life support for at least a few days until help arrives.

emergency supplies on hand

Would you be ready if a disaster struck your home? What if your basic services—water, gas, electricity—were cut off? The American Red Cross, the Canadian Red Cross, and the U.S. Federal Emergency Management Agency recommend always keeping a disaster supply kit on hand that contains the following items.

1 water

In a time of natural disaster, your water supply may be cut off or contaminated. To prepare for this situation, store about one gallon (4.5 ltrs) of water per person per day—you should store enough for three days. In hot environments or if you're likely to engage in physical activity, include an extra 2 qts (2 ltrs) per person per day. It is important to use plastic containers for storage, as other containers, such as milk cartons or glass bottles, may decompose or break. Remember to replace this water about every six months to ensure it's safe and clean to drink. If a disaster occurs, immediately store additional water in any other plastic containers you can find.

2 food

In the event you are unable to leave your house, you will need to have food supplies. Try to store at least a three-day supply of nonperishable items for the whole family. Foods that don't require refrigeration, preparation, or cooking are best, such as canned meats, fruits, vegetables, soups, or dried foods, such as crackers or cereals. Consider including vitamins and food supplements. You could have a small gas/camping stove available for heating up your food. Don't forget infant foods. Make sure you replace your supplies every six months so that they remain fresh.

3 first aid kit

Include different-sized sterile bandages and gauze pads, latex gloves, scissors, tweezers, a needle and strong thread, moistened towelettes, sunscreen, antiseptic, soap, a thermometer, and a tube of petroleum jelly. You should also include non-prescription drugs, such as aspirin, anti-diarrhea medication, and antacids, as well as any prescription medicines, such as asthma drugs, Epi-Pens (adrenaline shots), and insulin. Consult your pharmacist for advice on obtaining and storing prescription drugs. Remember family members with special requirements, such as infants and elderly people, who might need items like diapers, spare dentures, or an extra pair of eyeglasses.

4 tools and supplies

Make sure you are fully prepared for any disaster. Include plastic eating utensils and plates, a battery-operated radio and extra batteries, a flashlight, a utility knife with a can opener, a compass, signal flares, paper and pencil, matches in a waterproof container, a whistle, and a map of the area. Don't forget sanitation products, such as toilet paper, soap, personal hygiene items, disinfectant, household chlorine bleach, and plastic garbage bags.

5 clothing and footwear

Your kit should include a complete change of clothing and footwear for every family member. Make sure you have sturdy shoes or boots and waterproof clothing for everyone. Also include hats, gloves, and thermal underwear. Have at least two rescue blankets.

6 documents

Keep important documents, such as passports, insurance policies, and medical records, in a waterproof, portable, and preferably fireproof container. Make copies of everything and keep them in a safe deposit box or with a trusted friend or relative. Have a list of emergency numbers on hand along with enough cash to last a couple of weeks—this should include spare change.

if a disaster occurs

If you are told by the authorities to stay in your home, monitor local radio and television stations and follow the official advice. Close and lock all your windows and exterior doors, and block off any other places where air gets in, such as the fireplace damper. Remain calm. Check for injuries and give first aid, if required. Using a flashlight, not a naked flame, check for burst pipes. Sniff for gas leaks. Turn off the utilities, if necessary, and clear up any spilled flammable liquids. Call your emergency contact, then don't use the phone again, unless there is an emergency. Evacuate if advised to do so.

✔ PREPARE TO EVACUATE

Your evacuation kit is a smaller version of your household supply kit. If you have to leave your home, you won't have time to think about what you should include, so it's worth planning what to take now. Keep it in a large bag or trunk near your front door and make sure that each family member knows where to find it. Include the following:

☐ **Baby gear** Check that you have adequate food, diapers, bottles, and medications.

☐ **Bedding** Pack plenty of blankets and/or sleeping bags.

☐ **Candles** Take at least two 36-hour candles.

☐ **Cash** Make sure you have enough money to last you and the family for about two weeks. Include some small change.

☐ **Cell phone** Make sure you keep this charged.

☐ **Clothing** Pack at least one change of clothes for everyone along with sturdy boots and waterproof jackets.

☐ **Eating utensils** Include the same utensils as in your household supply kit.

☐ **First aid kit** Take the one from your household supply kit or create a duplicate kit.

☐ **Flashlight** Include extra batteries.

☐ **Other personal items** Add prescription medication, glasses, or dentures, according to your particular family's needs.

☐ **Radio** Get a radio that is portable and battery-powered to enable you to listen to official status reports following a disaster. Include an extra supply of batteries.

☐ **Toiletries** Include soap, toilet paper, and other personal hygiene items.

☐ **Utility knife** Make sure that this includes a can opener.

☐ **Water** Store enough for each family member to last three days (see opposite).

☐ **Whistle** Use this to attract attention.

helping others

How would you react if you found another person in danger? Would you intervene or walk away? If you decided to help, what would be the best way to go about it?

This book is about staying safe in all situations, no matter what. You shouldn't put yourself in danger to help someone else, but there are things you can do safely, such as phoning for help. Also, there are many long-term strategies you can adopt to help make your community a safer place to live.

do I have to help?

If you see someone in danger, you may think it's best not to get involved, and there are many valid reasons for this. You could get hurt; you might feel that it's not your responsibility; you could make matters worse; or you could get in the way. In the case of a crime, the police might think you were involved in some way. These are all good reasons to exercise caution but not to ignore a person in need of help.

being a Good Samaritan

Legally, in most countries, you are not required to help another person in danger. If you do nothing, you won't get into trouble. If you choose to help, however, you may be protected in the United States and Canada under so-called Good Samaritan laws. These laws were created to encourage people to help others in emergency situations, and they state that if you act sensibly and within your capabilities in an effort to save a life or prevent further injury, then you can't be held financially responsible for a victim's injuries. It's worth remembering, however, that Good Samaritan laws might not apply if you were "grossly or willfully negligent" when providing care.

There are certain circumstances in which the law might require you to offer help—if, for example, there is a "special relationship" between a bystander and the person in trouble, such as between an employer and employee or between a bus driver and a passenger. Another situation in which you might have to help is if you were responsible for placing the other person in danger—a motorist who has caused an accident will often be required to assist injured people and should, at the very least, make sure the emergency services are called. To find out about Good Samaritan laws in your area, contact a legal professional, search local legal Web sites, or visit your local library.

what can you do safely?

You may not want to get involved in a dangerous situation, but imagine how you would feel if you were in trouble and people were too scared to get involved. There are ways that you can help without putting yourself at risk. They are as follows:

- **PHONE FOR HELP** Tell the relevant emergency service exactly what is happening, who is

STREETSMART

STAY SAFE Helping others doesn't mean you have to go into a burning building or break up a fight—that might be the worst thing to do. If you get hurt you'll only make the situation harder for the next person who tries to help. When clear of danger, stop and think about what you can do. At the very least, call for emergency help.

involved, and the precise location. You should leave your name, but if there is some reason that you don't want to, an anonymous call is better than no call at all.

- **FIND A MEMBER OF THE STAFF** Look for anybody who works where you are, such as a security guard, club bouncer, teacher, train driver, or flight attendant.
- **SHOUT FOR HELP** Draw attention to the incident. If you are worried that others might ignore you, shout "fire!" (see page 72).
- **SHOUT AT AN ATTACKER** In the case of a fight or mugging, keep your distance but shout that you have called the police and they'll be there in a minute. Point out any closed-circuit TV cameras to the attacker so that he knows he is being filmed.
- **REMEMBER THE DETAILS** If a crime is being committed, write down a description of those involved so that you can inform the police and assist in identification at a later time.
- **WARN OTHERS** If you see someone heading for trouble, think of ways you could prevent it. For example, you could keep people clear of a burning building, or you could warn someone heading toward a group of drunks.

Good Samaritan laws encourage people to help others in emergency situations. If you act sensibly in your effort to save a life or prevent injury, you can't be held responsible for a victim's injuries.

take a long-term approach

You may think the police or the government are the only people responsible for safety on the streets; however, there is much we can all do to make our neighborhood a safer place. Whether your priority is the safety of your children or the safety of the community as a whole, you will find much in this book to help you protect the safety of yourself and others.

You might also like to take things further by joining a local initiative, a neighborhood watch program (see page 168), an action group such as the U.S.-based Brady Campaign to Prevent Gun Violence (see page 170), or a charity such as Prevent Child Abuse America (see page 169). If you suspect that a friend, neighbor, or family member is in any kind of danger, there are many societies and help lines that can offer practical advice. Some are listed on page 169. Your local library, police, and the Internet are also good sources of information.

2

situation safety

It's easy to overlook the hazards in our daily lives. Keep yourself and your possessions safe by improving your awareness in all situations—from walking down the street to surfing the Internet, from interacting with your work colleagues to going on vacation.

street safety

Street crime can happen at any time—day or night. According to research conducted by the U.S. Bureau of Justice Statistics, 54 percent of violent crimes occur between 6:00 A.M. and 6:00 P.M., and approximately two-thirds of sexual assaults occur at night between 6:00 P.M. and 6:00 A.M. It's up to you, therefore, to keep yourself and your belongings safe at all times.

stay alert
You should be constantly aware of your surroundings and anyone acting suspiciously. When you're out in public, try to avoid doing

things that will distract you, such as talking on your cell phone or rummaging in your bag. This can leave you vulnerable because your attention isn't focused on what's around you.

If possible, wait until you are in a safe environment, such as your office, to make calls or handle money.

As criminals often use the cover of darkness to launch an attack, it is wise to take extra precautions at night. No matter how good your vision, it is difficult to see clearly in the dark. If you are attacked, it can be hard to tell exactly what is happening or even how many attackers there are. At night the streets are generally quieter, meaning there are fewer people to witness an attack or come to a victim's aid. However, you can learn to protect yourself by taking the following steps.

use your fear
Fear causes the chemical adrenaline (see page 15) to be released in your body. This hormone will make you feel more alert, allowing you to watch and listen for potential dangers. To give yourself the best chance of seeing what's happening around you, stick to well-lighted areas. Also, because your sight may be compromised, you may find that your hearing improves slightly. If there aren't many people around, you'll be able to listen for footsteps or cars pulling up near you.

Wear your handbag over one shoulder or carry it in your hand. Don't wear it across your body—you risk injury if an attacker grabs it.

show positive body language

Attackers often watch people before they strike and evaluate them according to age, speed of movement, and general demeanor (see box, right). Knowing this, you can use your body language to convey a different message.

- **WALK CONFIDENTLY** Don't rush, but don't amble. Adopt a steady stride, with your head high and your shoulders back.
- **STAY ALERT** Don't look at the ground as you walk, but be attentive and look and listen to what is going on around you all the time. If somebody bumps into you or asks you for the time or a light, be aware that this may be a trick to distract you while somebody else picks your pocket.
- **PLAN YOUR ROUTE** Plan your journey in advance so you look confident and are sure of where you're going.
- **BE PREPARED** If you're not carrying anything, keep at least one hand out of your pocket—ready to defend yourself against an unexpected attack.

Stick to well-lighted streets and busy areas where there is less chance of an attack occurring.

dress wisely

Whenever possible, wear loose, comfortable clothing when you go out. You will be less vulnerable because you'll be able to move more quickly. Try not to wear expensive-looking jewelry or watches, which can make you a target. If you must wear them, be careful about

WHAT HAPPENS WHEN...

PICKPOCKETS CHOOSE THEIR VICTIMS

Most thieves want to avoid trouble and will use their criminal insight to evaluate a potential victim. They prefer to target somebody who is alone, distracted, timid, or drunk because that person will be easy to surprise and unwilling or unable to fight back. They may also evaluate a person's facial expression to detect how likely it is that the person will fight back.

what you do—if you are going to be coming home late, don't walk, but take a taxi. When you're in the street, cover up your jewelry with a scarf, gloves, or your sleeves.

be aware of others

The fear of being followed is much more common than the reality. However, you should never ignore your instincts (see page 15). Bear in mind the following advice.

know how to react

If you sense that someone is behind you, your immediate reaction may be to freeze, hoping the person will overtake you. But you must overcome these feelings.

> **Always turn to face your attacker. Facing him will give you a better picture of what is going on and will remove the element of surprise.**

Also, you will be able to assess the situation more accurately to see whether it is a false alarm or whether you are in danger. There may be more than one person, or you may see somebody carrying a weapon. All of these observations will help you decide how best to react. Turning around may even scare the person away because you will now be more able to identify your attacker at a later stage. Shouting and screaming may be enough to scare the person away—don't be embarrassed about getting it wrong.

don't get close to cars

If somebody in a car is driving slowly behind you as you walk, calling out of the window, or blowing the horn, it may just be meant as innocent fun. However, don't ignore the vehicle; it is always better to be safe than sorry. Look to

Overcome the instinct to freeze. If you turn to face an attacker, it will prevent him from placing a hand over your mouth and will allow you to scream if need be.

see who the driver is talking to and assess your situation: Can you tell what the driver wants? Can you change your route and walk away? Is there anyone around to help? How many people are in the car? One person is less of a threat than two or more.

If a driver asks you for directions, perhaps even opening a map, never get too close to the car. Stand more than an arm's length away, and shout the directions if you have to. If you feel at all nervous, say that you don't know and keep walking, glancing back occasionally to see what the driver is doing. If you are suspicious, walk in the opposite direction that the car is traveling

women feel more safe and secure on the street by taking note of these few simple guidelines:

- **CROSS THE STREET** Don't walk too closely behind a woman on her own—it can be very worrisome. Drop back a bit or walk on the other side of the street.
- **KEEP YOUR DISTANCE** Don't sit too close to a woman on a bus or in a train.
- **AVOID CONVERSATION** If it's late at night and you start talking to a lone female, she may not realize that you mean no harm.
- **BE CONSIDERATE** If you are with a group of male friends, don't stare, whistle, or talk to a lone woman. This can be very threatening.
- **HELP FEMALE FRIENDS** Offer a female work colleague or friend a ride home if it's late, or accompany her to the bus or train station.

look after your belongings

Muggers and pickpockets are everywhere. They can grab your bag before you know it; the element of surprise means they often get away easily. If you are carrying a backpack, don't put your wallet in the front pocket as this can be easily snatched. Also, be wary of anyone bumping into you or asking you a question. It might be a distraction ploy. A nearby accomplice could then snatch your belongings and escape with whatever he wants. If approached by a stranger, say "no" and keep walking in the direction of other people if you can. But don't turn your back to the stranger completely, as this makes you vulnerable.

know when to let go

If an attacker stops you and demands your money, watch, or jewelry, hand it over. Remember, your life is much more valuable than your possessions. If your bag is snatched, resist the urge to chase a thief. The most effective way

in; the driver would then have to reverse or turn around to follow you.

If a group of young men are trying to get your attention, shout at them to leave you alone and continue walking. Be firm and say it only once; don't get into a conversation, as they may see this as encouragement. If they get out and start coming after you, immediately go into a shop, restaurant, or anywhere there are other people. If you are on a residential street, go to the nearest house and knock on the front door—this is far less risky than staying on the street. Call the police and wait in safety.

moderate your behavior

For men, it can be difficult to realize that innocent actions can appear threatening to women. Men can play their part in helping

of retrieving your belongings and preventing him from attacking again is to keep a mental note of his appearance, your location, and the direction in which he is running. Report the incident as soon as possible.

card safety

Credit card fraud occurs in many ways, so it's important to protect your card at all times. Make sure you sign your card as soon as it arrives in the mail and always keep your personal identification number separate. After completing a transaction, keep your receipt in a safe place, as it will have your card details and signature on it. Also, when paying for items in shops or restaurants don't let a member of the staff take your card out of your sight. This is to make sure

Don't hold on if an attacker tries to snatch your bag. You could get injured in a pulling match, so just let go.

that your card details are not duplicated, which can then be used to commit fraud. Similarly, in a restaurant or bar, check your bill carefully and make sure you complete the total box, including any gratuity, before handing your card over. This ensures that no amount can be added to the bill after you've gone.

If you photocopy all the cards in your wallet, you can also minimize the damage if your wallet gets stolen. You will then have the

STREETSMART

BAG SENSE Keep handbags firmly zipped up or with the clasp facing your body. In a café or bar, try not to put your purse over the back of your chair. Instead, keep it in your lap or between your feet with one foot through the strap. In a restroom, don't put your purse on a hook where an arm could reach over and grab it.

account information on hand and can alert your credit card companies easily. You can also contact a U.S. national credit reporting organization, such as Equifax (see page 169), to place a fraud alert on your name and Social Security or Social Insurance number.

Be cautious when using your credit card to purchase items on the Internet. Order only from companies that are well known and have a solid reputation (see page 42).

situational awareness

Most people know to stay alert in unfamiliar situations. However, it is also vital to keep your wits about you in everyday situations. When you're leaving work, for example, you are usually tired and concentrating solely on getting home. It is also a regular journey, which can give you a false sense of security. However, don't let your guard down. Whenever you get ready to drive home from somewhere, go to the parking lot with a friend or colleague. Once in the car, stick to busy routes. If it's late or very early in the morning, consider taking a cab when you can—don't walk (see page 33).

shop safely

When leaving a shopping area, you won't be able to defend yourself and can make yourself a possible target for thieves if you are laden down with shopping bags. Try not to carry more than you can manage in one hand. If you've got a big shopping list, stop to relieve yourself of some of your packages by storing them in the trunk of your car.

According to Criminals Behind Bars—a support-based Web site for victims of crime (www.criminalsbehindbars.com), supermarket parking lots are one of the most dangerous

locations because you are often distracted as you load your car. If you are alone, avoid parking in quiet spots, even during daylight hours. Try to park as close to the store as possible, and if you have a lot of packages, ask a member of staff from the store to help load your car. In multistorey parking garages, avoid getting in elevators with lone males or using isolated stairwells. Always try to stay within sight and earshot of other people.

CHECK YOUR VALUABLES

When you go out, don't carry any unnecessary valuables. Be careful with the following:

☐ **Cell phone** If you have one, program it with numbers you would need in an emergency, including your home phone number.

☐ **Emergency numbers** Write down the 24-hour telephone numbers you need to cancel your credit cards, and carry them in a pocket.

☐ **Identification** Keep some form of ID on you in case your wallet is stolen and you need to prove your identity.

☐ **Keys** Keep your house keys in your hand or pocket—not in your bag. Plus, keep keys away from anything that lists your address.

☐ **Small change** Tuck a few spare coins or a phone card into a pocket in case you need to make a phone call to cancel your cards or phone a friend.

☐ **Wallet or purse** Keep the amount of money and the number of credit and debit cards to a minimum. Carry money in an inside or front pocket, which is less accessible to pickpockets. Always keep your checkbook separate from your credit cards.

Be alert when using an ATM, particularly at night—most attacks at ATMs occur between 7:00 P.M. and midnight. Always try to use a machine in a busy, public area and make sure no one is looking over your shoulder.

exercise wisely

Jogging and walking are great ways to relax and keep fit. However, as with other routines, it can be difficult to remain alert. Make sure you:

- **STAY AWARE** Don't run or walk wearing a personal stereo.
- **PICK A SENSIBLE TIME** Whenever possible, try to go out walking or jogging in daylight hours, when there are many people about.
- **GO AGAINST TRAFFIC** If you're on the roads, run or walk against the flow of traffic so that you can watch approaching cars.

be on guard while out in the open

On a summer's day, relaxing with friends and family, you can easily let your guard down. However, to stay safe, you must stay vigilant. If you visit a park or beach with children, try to stay in busy areas and watch what the other moms are doing. If they leave, take it as your cue to head home, too. Watch your children closely, and make sure that they understand the rules about talking to strangers (see page 136). Stay alert when you approach bushes and trees, as attackers will use these for cover.

Also, keep a close eye on your valuables. If you sleep or sunbathe, use your bag as a pillow with the zip or clasp closed, and if you get up to play a game or swim, make sure that somebody stays with the bags. To keep small valuables safe while swimming, place them in a waterproof tube, which can be worn around your neck. Many swimsuits also come equipped with zippered pockets to hold keys and cash.

travel wisely

After a hard day at work or a long night out, when you may be exhausted, it can be easy to get tunnel vision, with your sole objective being to get home and get to bed. Thinking about anything else may seem like a lot of effort. However, you must resist the urge to relax your mind or even fall asleep. Stay alert at all times, and watch what is going on around you, especially if you are on public transportation (see page 52). If you are on foot and you sense danger ahead, such as a group of drunk or unruly people, don't try to walk through them, but cross the street or take an alternate path.

know your route

On regular journeys, plan a route that is not only quick but also safe. Try out a few in the daytime to find the one that seems the best. In your mind, trace the route all the way from your front door to your destination. Consciously identify the danger zones, the areas that are poorly lighted or secluded, such as underpasses, remote bus stops, or empty train stations. If you are mentally prepared, you will feel more confident about walking through these areas. If there are lots of problem areas, look on a map to see if there is an alternative route you can take. Also, consider contacting your local authorities to ask for additional street lighting.

Pick out safe havens on your route, places where you can go for help if necessary, such as restaurants or stores—anyplace where there will be other people and you can call for help.

If you travel the route regularly, you may even become familiar with the faces or names of those who could help you. Don't become complacent once you have learned your route; treat every day as the first and stay safe.

On unfamiliar journeys, the rule about planning ahead still applies. Look at a map before you head out so that you don't have to stop for directions or fumble with a map. If you are on foot, try not to get too close to dark areas. On quiet streets, you can even walk in the road, which will mean that you're clear of bushes or doorways. Always walk facing the oncoming traffic—you will see vehicles approaching faster than someone stepping out of the darkness.

communicate your plans

People living with partners, family, or friends are often used to communicating their whereabouts, but it also is important to get into this habit if you live alone. If you go out, call a friend to let her know where you're going and

arrange to call again when you return. If people know where you should be, they can raise the alarm if something goes wrong. Don't forget to contact your friends or family if you decide to change your plans. Take a cell phone with you for this purpose.

share a ride

Whenever possible, arrange to travel home with friends or colleagues whom you trust. You can walk together, catch the same bus, or carpool. If you have to work late and can't leave at the same time, call a cab rather than take public transportation—some companies may even pay the fare for you. If you are going out for the evening, again, try to travel home with a friend.

Carry your keys in your hand when you are nearly home. Don't wait until you reach your doorstep, as fumbling in your bag can be an ideal distraction for an attacker.

use caution on evenings out

When going out with friends, you want to be able to enjoy yourself. However, you must still remain alert to potential theft or attack. Even at the movies, for example, if you leave your bag on the floor it can be an opportunity for a thief to steal it under the cover of darkness. The relaxing atmosphere in a bar or club can also lull you into a false sense of security. The social environment, combined with drinking, can cause you to lose your inhibitions and to talk to strangers more openly than you normally would. Remember also that alcohol can cause you and others to become more forward, excitable, or aggressive than normal, potentially leading to arguments or fights. The journey home, when it's dark and the streets are empty, can leave you more vulnerable to attack if you are not well prepared. To make sure that your nights out are safe and problem-free, you need to watch your behavior and keep your wits about you.

be wary of strangers

If you are chatting with somebody and decide that you don't want to continue the conversation, have an escape route planned. There is no need to be rude, but tell a white lie if you have to, such as, "Sorry, I'm waiting for somebody" or "My friends are looking for me." If somebody is actually pestering you, walk

Don't separate from your friends (right). If you get up to dance or talk with somebody else, always try to keep in view of your friends.

Don't leave valuables in sight (opposite) on the bar or table in front of you—it's too tempting for thieves. Keep them in your hand, in a pocket, or in a bag on your lap.

away and don't engage in conversation. Also, never go off to the restroom since it could give him a chance to get you alone.

A stranger may well be a friend you haven't yet met, but take your friendship slowly, particularly if you meet that person in a bar or club.

Be wary of giving out personal details, such as your full name or phone number. Even if your friends have met this person and have all of his details, it is no guarantee that the person is trustworthy. If you do decide to meet somebody again, ask for his phone number or arrange to meet in the daytime in a public place.

The rule that there is safety in numbers applies nowhere more than in a bar or club. Wherever you are, it's best to stick with a friend or group. Try to observe the following tips:

☐ **Plan ahead**   Consider how you are going to get home. Pre-book a taxi, or arrange a ride with a friend or a family member.

☐ **Arrange a meeting point**   Know precisely where you are going to meet. If you are going to be late, call ahead. If you are likely to be separated during the evening, arrange a time and a spot to return to at various points during the evening or before you go home. If possible, make your meeting point near doormen or security staff so that nobody is left waiting alone.

☐ **Guard your belongings**   One advantage of being with others is that you can have people watching many different directions at once. Keep an eye on each other's handbags, coats, and other belongings.

☐ **Stay together**   For women, going to the restroom together is not just sociable, it's much safer.

☐ **Stay sensible**   Don't let a group mentality go to your head. Keep your common sense, and don't let your friends persuade you to do something you wouldn't normally do.

☐ **Judge the mood**   If one of your group is getting pestered by a stranger, call to your friend to let the stranger know that she is not alone and to give her a chance to end the conversation. If a friend seems to be drunk, be prepared to take that person home.

☐ **Leave together**   Arrange to call each other when getting home. Make sure that everyone is able to get home safely. Stay at a friend's house if you are at all nervous about traveling home alone—you'll be more awake and thus safer if you wait until morning. Never leave a friend behind.

avoid confrontations

According to a report cited by the U.S. National Institute on Alcohol Abuse and Alcoholism, 37 percent of assault offenders and 60 percent of sexual offenders were drinking at the time that they committed an offense. Violence in drink-oriented surroundings is common. This is because alcohol disrupts thought processes and can cause people to behave impulsively, to misjudge situations, and to become more aggressive than usual.

For this reason, you need to be particularly aware of other people's behavior in a bar. If you bump into somebody or vice versa, apologize if necessary and go on your way. If someone upsets you, control your own anger, and try not to get into an argument. If the person persists and starts to hassle you or a friend, just walk away. Try not to let an argument progress into a fight; seek help from staff or security.

If a fight breaks out near you, you can help by alerting security; don't try to break it up yourself, as you may suffer injuries or be asked to leave.

If you are worried that there may be troublemakers waiting outside for you, stay in the building and call a cab. When it arrives, ask security to watch or escort you to the cab. This may mean waiting an extra 20 minutes, but it is worth it for peace of mind. Remember, it is always a good rule at the end of the evening to go home immediately. Don't hang around outside a bar or club because this is where many fights or assaults occur.

Travel home with a friend. Make sure that you have a trusted friend to travel home with. If she travels farther in the cab alone, ask her to phone you when she arrives home safely.

Keep your drink in sight. If you do have to leave your glass or bottle, make sure that somebody you trust is watching it. If you are unsure, buy another.

watch your drinks

Drugs and alcohol have long been used to sedate victims of sexual assault. However, the last decade has seen a new awareness of so-called date-rape drugs. From newspaper stories you may be familiar with such names as Rohypnol and gamma-hydroxybutyrate (GHB). The first of these is a sleeping pill that is illegal in the United States and Canada but can be obtained on the black market. GHB was formerly used by bodybuilders to increase their body mass and was once widely available in health food stores. Its availability is now strictly regulated in North America.

These and other drugs have been used by sexual offenders because of the effects they produce. Individuals react differently, but the possible effects include impaired judgment, loss of inhibitions, dizziness, confusion, lack of coordination, drowsiness, and loss of memory. These drugs may also be colorless, odorless, and tasteless, which is why you can never be too careful about what you're drinking when you're socializing. Protect yourself with these tips:

- **BUY YOUR OWN DRINKS** Don't accept drinks from a stranger. Only accept drinks directly from serving staff. If you want to accept one from a stranger, go to the bar with him and watch the drink being poured.
- **KEEP DRINKS SEPARATE** Don't share drinks with anyone. Avoid drinking punches at parties.
- **FIND A SAFE PLACE** If you experience any of the symptoms mentioned or feel nauseous, find a friend or a member of security or the management and get to a safe place. Call the police. Try to get a sample of the drink.
- **STAY ALERT** Be aware of the behavior of your friends. If someone starts to act strangely or feel ill, stay with her and get to a safe place. Again, talk to the management, call an ambulance if necessary, and try to get a sample of the drink.

watch your food

Aside from the behavior of others, one of the more common hazards you might encounter while in a public place is food poisoning. Avoid an upset stomach or more serious illnesses by following a few precautions. Where possible, choose well-established restaurants. Check the general condition of the restaurant environment. Are the floors, tables, and utensils clean? Do the cooks and serving staff look hygienic with short or tied-back hair and clean clothes and hands? Is your food properly heated through? If you do get food poisoning, contact the restaurant or make a formal complaint to the U.S. Food Safety and Inspection Service or the Canadian Food Inspection Agency (see page 170).

safeguard your home

Everybody—whether young or old, single or living with others—needs to feel safe in his own home. With good home security you can feel confident that you and your family, along with your possessions and property, are protected.

protect your stuff

Take some time to think about your possessions and how best to protect them. Whether they are worth money or only of sentimental value, you'll still want to safeguard them.

mark your possessions

Permanently marking your possessions in a visible and unique manner will help to deter burglars and make it easier for police to return items to you if they are recovered. Use an indelible ink pen to mark the back or bottom of the item. Write your ZIP or postal code, address, and last name so that you can be identified and the item returned. Or use an ultraviolet (UV) pen. This creates a mark that can be read only under a special handheld lamp, to which the police will have access. Because the markings are invisible, they will not actively deter burglars. However, it does mean your property can be identified if it's recovered. Bear in mind that UV markings fade with time, so they will need to be reapplied every six months.

You can help police to identify stolen items by taking photographs of valuable possessions and by keeping a list of all serial numbers. This will also help for insurance purposes.

Engrave valuable items using a scalpel or electric engraving pen—available from large hardware stores. Local law enforcement agencies also may offer an engraving service or lend you equipment.

insure against theft

Taking out a homeowners' insurance policy will prevent a burglary from turning into a financial disaster. Remember to separately list expensive items on your homeowners' insurance. Insurers will tell you the amount in value that needs to be insured separately and will ask for receipts and serial numbers if you have them. If you don't do this and you lose a valuable item, the insurer may refuse to pay you. Get into the habit of keeping receipts for all household purchases in a safe place.

create a safe house

Locking doors and windows and installing alarm systems can go a long way toward making you feel secure, but you should also think beyond your house and consider your yard or grounds and the community as a whole. For information on home security devices, see page 40.

keep grounds and yards safe

Always keep tools and ladders locked up to prevent intruders from using them to break into your premises. Also, maintain any fences surrounding your property. Not only will this prevent easy access to your house, but a strong fence can make it difficult for intruders to remove property, such as TVs or stereos.

Outdoor lighting that comes on automatically when darkness falls acts as a useful deterrent. Passive infrared lighting is another option, with the light activated by movement in its field of vision. Both types can be purchased from home improvement stores and are simple to install. These lights make it easier for you to see what is in your yard and also help create the impression that the house is occupied when you are out.

A cheap and effective way to make your home more secure is to place prickly and thorny plants in strategic spots in your garden. Thorny climbing plants, such as roses, not only look pretty but can also make fences difficult to climb. Holly is a good choice of plant to make downstairs windows less vulnerable.

Try laying gravel along driveways and paths, or even underneath windows and around the sides of the house, since walking on gravel makes a lot of noise, and you will be able to hear an unwelcome intruder.

enlist neighbors

Your neighbors are in the best position to keep an eye on your home when you are away, to notice anything suspicious, and to watch out for your safety. Get to know your neighbors, and let them know about any particular concerns you might have. Ask them to check on you if they think anything may have happened and to call the police if they think you may be in trouble. Many areas run neighborhood watch programs to encourage communities to look out for each other and build relationships with local law enforcement agencies (see page 168).

Local police and government departments often offer talks on safety, pamphlets describing crime patterns, or programs offering door chains or peepholes for older people. The police prefer to prevent crime from happening in the first place, so it's worthwhile to contact your local police department about this. In addition, the U.S. Department of Justice and the Canadian National Crime Prevention Centre run various national community programs, which are detailed on their Web sites (see page 169).

DEFEND AGAINST INTRUDERS

One of the things that people fear most is finding an intruder in the house. It's important to remember, however, that he is more likely to want to steal your possessions than harm you. If you find an intruder...

☐ **Call the police** If you have a phone in your bedroom, call the police immediately. Don't go to investigate the noise.

☐ **Stay out of sight** Don't be tempted to confront the intruder, who may become violent if cornered or frightened.

☐ **Make a noise** You may be able to scare off your intruder by making a noise, such as flushing the toilet or slamming a door.

☐ **Defend yourself** Despite reports of intruders suing people who try to fight them off, you may be justified in defending yourself if you fear harm.

☐ **Get out** If you can sneak out of the house, go immediately to a neighbor, and if you have not done so already, call the police.

install safety features

There are lots of ways to make your home more secure. One of the most important is to ensure that all outside doors on your property are fitted with secure locks.

> If your keys are lost or stolen, breaking into your home can be expensive. Have spare sets of house and car keys made, and keep them in a safe place with a relative or trusted neighbor.

Remember that the back door is vulnerable too. Often, it is hidden from the street, giving a thief more time to force entry. Here are some other security devices to help protect your home (see also page 156):

- **DOOR JAMMERS** These are sturdy, steel poles that can be jammed under the handle of a hinged door or, with the ends removed, placed along the inside track of a sliding door frame.

WHAT HAPPENS WHEN...

BURGLARS TARGET YOUR HOUSE

Research conducted by the U.S. Metropolitan Burglar and Fire Alarm Association shows that burglars take about 30 to 40 minutes to choose their target. They will usually pick a familiar neighborhood and look for a secluded family home near a main street. The most frequent hours to break in are between 9:30 A.M. and 4:00 P.M. when family members are likely to be at work or school. The front and back doors and first-floor windows are the most common points of entry. Once in the house, thieves head immediately for the bedroom as this is where most of us keep our valuables. They are looking for easy-to-carry items, such as jewelry or a camera that can be sold for cash.

- **WINDOW LOCKS** All ground-floor windows, and those that can be reached by climbing, should be fitted with locks. Remember, it's easier for an intruder to enter through a window than through a strong door. Lock small windows, too; even if a window cannot be climbed through, an intruder could reach through it and force open a larger window. You can also buy protective metal window covers, which are very secure as they are bolted into the brickwork and cannot be pulled out easily.

- **ALARMS** There are two main types of house alarms you can buy: an audible system, which will sound an alarm when activated—when movement sensors are triggered—and silent alarms, which alert a 24-hour security company or the local police station.

- **LIGHT SWITCHES FITTED WITH TIMERS** If you are out for the night, setting lights to switch on at different times during the evening will create the impression that someone is home. It is even possible to fit motors to your curtains so that when you are away they are still opened and closed.

- **SAFES** Consider a safe for valuable items or documents. Some are burglar-resistant, others are fire-resistant, and a few are both. Safes built into the floor offer the best protection. However, if you can't afford a safe, wrap your jewelry or valuables in a cloth and hide them in the attic, out of immediate sight.

- **EXTRA PHONES** Install a phone socket in the bedroom. Or if you have a cell phone, leave it by your bedside at night where it is easy to grab in an emergency. Also, fit a dead bolt lock on your bedroom door to stop an intruder from entering and to give you time to call the police.

protect your doors

Some of the first targets for illegal entry into your home are the front and back doors, so it's important to make them as burglarproof as possible.

Remember, if you do lock the door from the inside, you should always keep the key in the lock or on a nearby shelf, so that it is easily accessible in an emergency, such as a fire.

1 STURDY DOOR Exterior doors should be made of solid timber, and shouldn't be less than 1¾ in. (4.5 cm) thick. Ensure they are supported by three hinges at least 4 in. (10 cm) wide.

2 CYLINDER LOCK Fit an automatic dead-latch cylinder lock. This should be placed about a third of the way down the door.

3 DEAD-BOLT LOCK Fit a dead-bolt lock about a third of the way up the door. The rigid construction inside these locks makes them stronger than locks that are operated by a spring action. Double cylinder dead-bolt locks need to be locked from the inside with a key to make them effective; make sure you keep the key nearby to allow easy escape in case of fire.

4 DOOR FRAME The frame should be made of solid timber and securely bolted to the walls. It is a good idea to strengthen it by fitting a metal bar to support all the locking points.

5 PANELS If your door has recessed panels, they should be at least ⅓ in. (1.5 cm) thick in order to prevent someone from sawing through this part of the door.

6 PEEPHOLE Install this at eye level and don't forget to use it. Make sure you also have a porch light so that you can use the peephole at night.

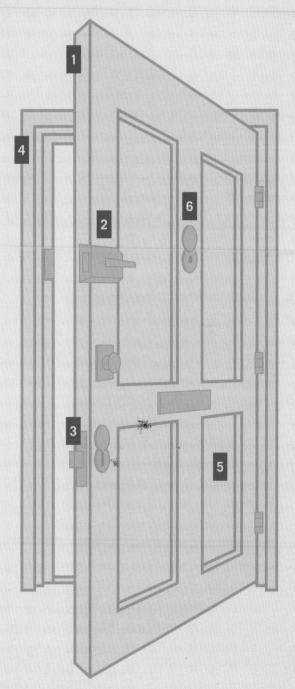

stay safe in cyberspace

The Internet revolution has provided a wealth of opportunities for exchanging information and ideas. Unfortunately, it has also created opportunities for those who want to con others. The International Web Police–a U.S. based agency dedicated to protecting the Internet community–estimates that computer crime may cost as much as $50 billion per year, largely due to stolen software and fraud. For parents with children using the Internet, there are concerns also about safe access–knowing what their kids are downloading or whom they are talking to.

Protecting your computer is important. If somebody can access your files, he will not only be able to read personal information but will also be able to charge his own Internet use to your phone bill. Keep your files safe:

- **CHANGE YOUR PASSWORD** Choose a new one regularly. Make sure it is nothing obviously connected to you, such as a family name or birthday. The best passwords are a mixture of numbers and letters, upper- and lower-case.
- **KEEP IT A SECRET** Memorize your password. Try not to write it down, or if you do, keep it well away from your computer.
- **TRY NOT TO SAVE IT** If your computer or a Web site gives you the option of saving your password, don't take it. If anyone uses your computer, he will have access to every place you have saved a password.
- **BE WARY** If you receive an e-mail claiming to be from your Internet provider asking for your password, it is a scam–do not respond.

how do I shop safely?

The Internet is great for shopping from the comfort of your own home, giving you a wider range of goods than you could ever hope to find in your local area. However, you do need to be very careful of how you go about it. According to the International Web Police, the cost to credit card insurers of stolen credit card numbers has been estimated at more than

Keep the computer in the open, where everybody can access it and you can keep an occasional check on what your children are looking up.

$3 billion. If you don't know about or trust a company, ask for a hard copy of its catalog before you purchase anything, or check with the consumer protection agency or department in your state or province about whether the company is licensed or registered. Shop around a little before you commit to buying. If something seems like an unbelievable deal, then it probably is. Double-check the small print for hidden costs before you commit—look at the total price, the delivery dates, the return and cancellation policies, and the guarantee.

Only enter sensitive information, including your credit card details, when you are in a secure site (see box, opposite). If you are unsure, call the company and pay over the phone or by check. When you do enter your information, don't enter more than is necessary—giving out too much personal information puts you at risk of falling prey to a con artist, as well as receiving extra junk mail.

is it OK to chat?

Chat rooms allow you to take part in real-time conversations with people from anywhere in the world. They can be interesting, fun, and very informative but also have their risks. Although monitors from the site sometimes check on content, there are a couple of things you should look out for. First, anyone who is logged on can read what you are writing, so you should resist the temptation to say things you wouldn't normally say in public. Second, keep your identity a secret. Don't include your real name, address, or phone number in a chat room, but use an alias. Finally, take action if you are upset by what you read. If someone is using offensive language, leave. You can report that person to your Internet provider, giving the time, the name of the chat room, and her screen name.

PROTECT YOUR KIDS

Although parents can monitor their children's progress at school, it is difficult to supervise their Web activity. Here are a few tips that will help:

☐ **Use appropriate screen names** Police say this is the first defense against Internet predators. Names such as "soccerboy12" can attract unsavory contact. Also, don't incorporate personal information into a screen name and don't submit profiles.

☐ **Be available** Take an interest in what your children are looking up, and encourage them to tell you about anything that makes them feel uncomfortable.

☐ **Limit their access** Tell your kids exactly how long they can spend on the Internet. If they have only a limited time to do research, they should be more focused on looking up what they need. Tell them not to enter any personal information on a site, and warn them about the dangers of chatting online.

☐ **Look up the history** If you are concerned about the sites that your child or teen has been using, there are ways of finding every site that has been visited. You should look for "history," which can be located on most computers by going into the Internet and looking at the toolbars at the top or left of the page or pressing "ctrl" and "h." If you need additional help, go to the help page.

☐ **Discover blocking, filtering, and rating** There are various ways of blocking access to Web sites that you consider unsuitable. Some methods block or filter out sites based on language or images; others prevent users from entering personal information or using e-mail or chat rooms. Contact your Internet service provider for information, investigate the tools available on your browser, or perform a search on "family filters" or "blocking."

☐ **Contact the school** If you are concerned about your children's access at school, ask to see the school guidelines on Internet use.

safety in the workplace

Most of us spend a great deal of our adult lives in the workplace without giving any thought to safety issues. If you work in a high-risk environment, such as a construction site or with machinery, you should receive special safety training from your employer. However, even in an office environment, there are laws governing safe working conditions, and a copy of all regulations should be displayed on a bulletin board. For advice on dealing with inappropriate behavior from work colleagues, see page 46.

prevent accidents

In 2000, according to the U.S. National Safety Council, nearly 4 million U.S. citizens suffered disabling injuries while at work and over 5000 were killed. In Canada, according to the Canadian Centre for Occupational Health and Safety, 800,000 people are injured and 800 die each year. All workplaces have a legal obligation to ensure the safety of their employees. However, safety is the responsibility of everyone, and you need to do all you can to

check your office workstation

Reduce the risks of eye strain, fatigue, and musculoskeletal injuries, such as tendonitis or carpal tunnel syndrome, by checking your posture and practices at your computer.

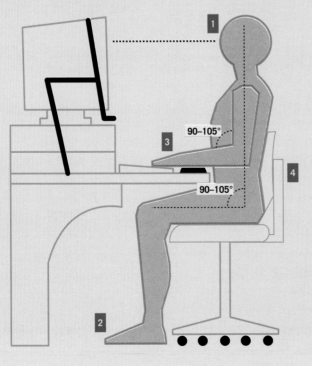

1 EYES Adjust your seat so that your eyes are level with the topmost line of your computer screen.

2 FEET Put your feet flat on the floor or use a footrest so that your knees are at right angles to your body.

3 WRISTS Check that your wrists are level with your hands while typing. Use a wrist pad, if necessary.

4 BACK Make sure your lower back is always fully supported by your chair.

5 GENERAL Stand up and take regular breaks at least every hour to stretch your legs and rest your eyes.

ensure that your work environment is safe. These measures will vary according to your type of employment and so can range from keeping computer cords tucked out of the way to making sure dangerous chemicals are locked up. For in-depth information on safety issues in the workplace, contact either the U.S. Occupational Safety and Health Administration (www.ohsa.gov) or the Canadian Centre for Occupational Health and Safety (www.ccohs.ca).

check first aid supplies

All workplaces should have a well-stocked first aid kit on the premises. It should be relevant to the kind of work; for example, if you work in a kitchen, you should have ice packs in case of burn injuries. The quantity of first aid kits available will depend on the number of employees. The kits must be easily available and their locations known to staff members. All workplaces, whatever their size, should have an employee trained in first aid on the premises.

prepare for emergencies

The disasters you could face at work are similar to those that you could face anywhere, whether at home or in public. However, considering how much time you spend at work, it is worth thinking about your employer's plans and responsibilities in case of a fire, natural disaster, structural damage, or terrorist action.

All employers should have emergency plans in place. These should include training individuals or teams to deal with fire marshaling, first aid, and even bomb searches. A designated chain of command must be communicated to all staff outlining each person's individual responsibilities. Safety

✓ CHECK FOR SUSPICIOUS MAIL

As the bioterrorism following September 11, 2001, illustrated, the postal system can be used as an effective vehicle for spreading illness. When examining mail, consider the following areas:

☐ **Address** Consider if this is handwritten or poorly typed, possibly with misspelled words.

☐ **Discolorations** Look out for oily stains or a powdery substance on the wrapper.

☐ **Postage** Check for excessive postage or none at all. Look also for foreign stamps.

☐ **Restrictive markings** Be wary of phrases like "confidential," "personal," or "do not X-ray."

☐ **Return address** Look for a return address that is different from the postmarked location.

checks should be carried out on a regular basis to see whether alarms are present, operational, effective, and understood by all.

All evacuation routes should be clearly posted, well-lighted, and clear of obstructions. Even if these are not your direct responsibilities, you owe it to yourself to adhere to all safety guidelines and report any problems with the emergency plans, such as blocked exits or faulty fire alarms.

Keep fire doors closed at all times. They are placed to prevent a fire from spreading quickly through a building, giving people time to escape.

Take it upon yourself to find out your designated assembly point in case of evacuation. Also, take 10 minutes out of your day to learn about the different types of firefighting equipment available, such as smoke blankets and fire extinguishers.

When an alarm sounds, take the situation seriously and follow any instructions given. Try not to panic at any time. Even if you smell smoke or see structural damage, stay calm as you vacate the premises. Also, keep in mind the following fire safety guidelines:

- **GET OUT** Leave the building immediately.
- **DON'T STOP** Don't waste time collecting personal belongings.
- **AVOID ELEVATORS** Do not use the elevators. Elevators can cease to operate, and elevator shafts can fill with smoke in a fire.
- **HELP OTHERS** Help a colleague if necessary, or request help from emergency personnel.
- **GO TO THE ASSEMBLY POINT** Meet outside at the allocated assembly point so marshals can conduct a head count. If you walk away before being told it is safe to do so, you may cause emergency services personnel to enter the building unnecessarily.
- **DON'T GO BACK** Never return to a building until told it is safe to do so.

BE ALERT TO BULLIES

Identifying a bully can be difficult because the culprit can be subtle. If you are a human resources manager or an employer, look out for the following signs among employees:

- ☐ **Ostracized workers** Other workers as well as the bully may avoid associating with a victim.
- ☐ **Persistent criticism** This may be both personal and work-related.
- ☐ **Sickness levels** There may be high absenteeism, perhaps in one department only.
- ☐ **Staff morale** This may be low and workers may lack initiative.
- ☐ **Unusual workloads** One worker may have responsibilities taken away or be given impossible tasks or deadlines.

maintain good relationships

Feeling intimidated, threatened, or undermined by a work colleague can make the workday unbearable. Bullying is prevalent in some workplaces and may even form part of the culture. If you are the one being bullied, here is an action plan:

- **CONFRONT THE BULLY** Use statements such as "I find that comment offensive" or "Could you tell me why I was excluded from that meeting?" He might be embarrassed into rethinking his behavior or genuinely may not have realized the behavior was offensive.
- **SEND A WRITTEN WARNING** If the bullying continues, back up your words with a written message delivered to the bully. And send a copy of the message to your human resources department or employer.
- **KEEP A RECORD** Detail the incidents of bullying. Present the information to your supervisor, human resources staff, or union representative. Most employers will have procedures in place to put a stop to it.
- **SEEK GUIDANCE** Go to the U.S. Equal Employment Opportunity Commission or the Canadian Human Rights Commission (see page 170) if you are being bullied by your boss and don't receive the help you think you should.

prevent sexual harassment

Both men and women can be victims of sexual harassment in the workplace, and it can make an individual feel threatened and unsafe. Sexual harassment includes all forms of unwanted sexual conduct, such as lewd jokes, fondling, name calling, and repeated requests for dates or sexual favors. There may be the implication that this behavior should be reciprocated in return for promotion, pay raises, or better working

conditions. Such behavior can seriously affect an individual's dignity and create a hostile, intimidating work environment.

Unfortunately, it's sometimes difficult to identify these feelings because workplace cultures vary enormously. It can be common for strong language, sexual banter, or even physical contact to be excused as a joke or as part of normal office life. However, this does not mean you should have to contend with inappropriate behavior. If actions or comments make you feel uncomfortable, follow the same procedure as you would when dealing with a bully: confront the person as soon as you can and keep a detailed record of incidents. Keep copies of any warnings you have given to the person who is harassing you. Then present the information to your supervisor, human resources manager, or union representative.

Remember, most employers take a claim of sexual harassment very seriously and will have

Sexual harassment at work can make you feel threatened. Speak to the individual concerned first—he might be embarrassed into stopping his behavior. Keep a detailed record of incidents. Then tell your supervisor.

a complaint process to follow. If you do not receive the help you think you should, or are being harassed by your boss, consult a lawyer.

guard against violence

A violent attack can occur anywhere, and work is no exception. There is no excuse for violent behavior, and attacking a colleague is a cause for instant dismissal and, in many cases, should be reported to the police. The environment, hours, and area in which you work may present more risks. However, there is no need to feel vulnerable. Talk to your employer about safety procedures. If you are working nights, for example, your employer may help to ensure you get home safely.

auto safety

A car can give you a good deal of independence and security: You are in control of when and where you go and whether you take anyone with you. You can lock the doors and shut others out and easily take a trip without being in contact with anyone else. Unfortunately, though, the way we behave when driving can lead to violence—the much reported "road rage" of recent years. Although you cannot control the actions of others, you can do a lot to avoid both conflict and accidents on the road.

avoid accidents

According to the U.S. National Safety Council, motor vehicle crashes cause a death every 12 minutes. And Transport Canada estimates that almost 200,000 Canadians have perished on the road in the last 50 years. Yet many of us believe that an accident will never happen to us. Although you cannot plan for every occurrence, caring for your car and practicing safe driving can go a long way toward reducing your risks of being involved in an accident.

drive safely

Accidents can occur anywhere, at any time, and for hundreds of reasons. The best way to deal with the unpredictable is to drive defensively—anticipating problems and being prepared. Follow the obvious precautions, such as slowing down when you approach intersections or whenever children are around, but also consider these points:

- **STAY FOCUSED** Avoid all possible distractions. Never talk on, or attempt to answer, a cell phone while in the car. If you need to check a map, stop to do so.

Maintain a safe distance. For every 10 mph (16 km/h) of speed, stay one vehicle length from the car in front. In bad conditions, or at high speeds, double this distance.

- **WEAR A SEAT BELT** In 1999, the U.S. National Highway Traffic Safety Administration (NHTSA) calculated that more than 9500 deaths could have been prevented by the use of safety belts. Similar research conducted by Transport Canada shows that from 1990 to 1997, 8600 drivers and front passengers in Canada were saved by seat belts. Belts are required by law in all states and provinces.
- **STAY ALERT** The NHTSA has calculated that about 70,000 car accident injuries are a result of fatigue. Tiredness is far more likely to cause problems on extended, high-speed journeys. At the first signs of tiredness, stop, take a 20-minute nap, and drink a coffee. On longer journeys, share the driving.
- **CONTROL THE KIDS** If you are driving with children, try to keep a reasonable level of discipline, and make sure that they are properly strapped in, even for short trips.

If you are using child safety seats, check that you have fitted the correct type for your children (www.nhtsa.dot.gov), and ask your local police station to check that they are correctly installed.

■ **TAKE RESPONSIBILITY** Safety features, such as air bags and antilock brakes, can prove life-saving in an accident. However, technology is no substitute for safe driving. In fact, tests at the United Kingdom's Transport Research Laboratory suggest that car safety features tend to encourage "risk compensation"; that is, drivers may tend to relax more behind the wheel and risk becoming careless.

avoid road rage

A recent survey by the American Automobile Association revealed that almost 90 percent of motorists had felt "road rage" at some point when driving. In Canada, according to PDE Publications, an organization that studies driver behavior, 85 percent of Canadians said they'd engaged in aggressive driving in 2000. Fortunately, most people don't act on that rage. For some, however, it turns into an

overwhelming anger that causes them to drive aggressively and dangerously or even to attack other drivers. Protect yourself against road rage by learning how to control anger in yourself and how to avoid others who have it.

Getting stressed by other drivers means you are more likely to get involved in an argument. Try not to get annoyed if somebody slows you down—always allow plenty of time for your journey. If you're upset with another driver, don't shout or gesture, and avoid eye contact, which could be interpreted as a direct challenge. Instead, take a deep breath and cool down. Listen to soothing music if you find that it helps you to relax.

Always be considerate of other drivers. Don't drive too closely behind the car in front, and if someone is tailgating you, let him pass. Make sure that you signal properly before you change lanes or turn, and don't do so abruptly. If you cut someone off accidentally, mouth the word "sorry" or raise your hand as an apology.

In the unlikely event that a person is deliberately targeting you with his aggressive driving, don't ever be tempted to stop. Drive to the nearest service station and call the police.

▌STREETSMART

DON'T DRINK AND DRIVE And don't get into a car with someone who has been drinking. Transport Canada reports that impaired drivers continue to account for 32 percent of all driver fatalities. If you suspect another driver is drunk, pull over to let him pass. Stop and call the police and let them know the make of the car and license plate.

coping with car problems

If you have problems with your car and need to stop, pull over to the side of the road but try to stay in your vehicle. If you have a cell phone, call for assistance. Tie a white handkerchief or something similar to the door handle or antenna as this will signal to passing police that you need help. If you have to leave your car to call

PREVENT CARJACKING

Although carjacking remains relatively rare, the U.S. Department of Justice suggests that it is on the increase. Make sure you are not a victim of this crime by following these steps:

☐ **Be alert** When approaching your car, be wary of people nearby.

☐ **Have your keys ready** Carry your keys in your hand so that you do not waste time when unlocking the door to get in.

☐ **Lock the doors** Get into the habit of locking your car doors as soon as you get in, even if you are with others.

☐ **Be cautious when parking** Check out your surroundings before you get out of your car and look for anyone unusual hanging around.

☐ **Leave room to maneuver** When stopped in traffic, always leave enough room from the car in front of you to be able to drive around it. Don't get boxed in. If you are approached by a stranger while in the car, don't open your doors or windows.

☐ **Take action** If you feel threatened, sound your horn continuously to scare any potential carjackers away. However, if you are being threatened with a weapon, give up the car and get away quickly.

for help, always lock the doors, even if the engine is not working. When you contact the emergency road crew, tell them if you are a lone female or with children so that they will treat you as a priority. It is worth investing in a warning triangle to alert other drivers that there is a stopped vehicle in their path. Place it about 150 ft. (45 m) behind your vehicle, and return to the car to wait for the emergency road crew to arrive. Lock all your doors, and if a stranger stops to help you, don't open the doors or windows to speak to him. Thank the person, but say that you are waiting for the police.

what to keep in your car

Preparation can make all the difference in the event of a breakdown. The most obvious items to have in the car are a cell phone, a blanket, and a flashlight. However, a tool kit is useful also, including items such as pliers, a wrench, a jack, spare fuses and headlight bulbs, electrical tape, a length of light wire, battery jump-start cables, and a spare tire.

Keep a first aid kit on hand similar to the one that you would keep in the house (see page 20), and consider keeping a fire extinguisher in your car. This is useful for putting out small fires, but in the event of an engine fire or a fire that looks as if it could spread, get away from the car.

prevent theft

In the United States, a car is stolen every 20 seconds, according to the U.S. Insurance Information Institute. The Vancouver Police Department says that Canada has experienced a 74 percent increase in car theft during the last 10 years, making its rate of car theft now higher than in the U.S. This crime costs victims time and money and ultimately forces insurance premiums to rise.

Don't make it easy for thieves to take your car. On top of locking it and parking in well-lighted streets, turn the wheels to the side when parking to prevent the car from being towed by thieves. In parking lots where you are given a ticket, take it with you when you leave the car.

Keep a record at home of your car's vehicle identification number (VIN), which can be found on a metal plate on the dashboard. VINs of stolen vehicles are registered with the FBI and the Canadian Police Information Centre.

don't stop

There are many situations in which somebody might try to stop you when driving. But the general rule is: Don't stop. This might be obvious with hitchhikers, but it also applies to breakdown situations and accidents you may encounter. One ploy that carjackers often use is to pretend they have a flat tire. Even if you see an accident, don't stop; drive on until you see a a safe place to stop and phone for help.

If someone bumps you from behind, be wary; this is another known trick of carjackers. Stop, but don't get out; let the other driver approach you. Keep your doors locked, and open your window only slightly to speak to him. Be ready to drive away. If you do drive away, report the accident and your concerns to the police.

Visual deterrents, such as a removable car radio (far left), or a lock that fits to the steering column, (left), may put off opportunist thieves. Besides the antitheft devices fitted by the manufacturer, you can also install some devices yourself. Consider: alarms; vehicle tracking systems; immobilizer switches that interrupt the fuel or electronic systems; and locks for the gas cap, wheels, or batteries. You can purchase these antitheft devices from most auto parts stores.

protection on public transportation

On a regular commute, it can be easy to slip into a false sense of security in familiar surroundings. However, public transportation provides many opportunities for attackers. This is why you should stay alert at all stages of your trip, including ordering your cab, waiting for your train, traveling in a subway car, or leaving a station.

stay alert on buses and trains

For some, taking public transportation is a part of everyday life. It can feel so routine that it is hard to imagine that you are putting yourself at risk. However, it can make you vulnerable to attacks from strangers. For one thing, you are outside the relatively controlled environment of your house, office, or car. Furthermore, a bus or train may be crowded, and you are likely to be distracted at certain points, such as when buying a ticket or passing through a barrier, giving a pickpocket a perfect chance to strike. At other times you may find yourself isolated and trapped, limiting the chance that somebody could come to your assistance. When using buses, trains, or subways, you are also likely to be tired from either a day at work or a night out. For all of these reasons, never let your guard down.

find a safe place to wait

When waiting, choose to stand in a well-lighted area. If you feel anxious about the other people waiting near you, make sure you get on another car or sit by the driver. However, if you think you will still be vulnerable hail a cab. If you are on a train or subway platform, stand near the exit in case trouble starts. Waiting near the end of a platform that has no entrances or exits

Know the timetable of your bus or train. Minimize your waiting time by turning up just five minutes before it's due. This will help ensure that there are other people waiting when you get there.

Sit near the driver on buses. He will be aware of any trouble that may start and will be able to call for police assistance, if necessary.

nearby can leave you trapped. Also, avoid standing too close to the edge of a platform, particularly in crowds when somebody could bump into you.

sit with others

Most of us know that it's not a good idea to sit in a train or subway car alone at night, but this is also a good rule to follow in the daytime. Try to sit in an area with a mixture of old and young men and women, and avoid sitting near lone males or large, boisterous groups. If everyone else has left the train or bus, leaving you alone, wait to see who gets on at the next stop. If a lone male gets on, get off or use the connecting doors to move to a car with more people inside. If you're on a bus, try to sit near the driver. He will be able to radio for assistance if necessary. Also, find the nearest stop button. If you do get into trouble, press it repeatedly and shout to get people's attention. Stay alert at all times—and most important, don't fall asleep.

exit safely

Wait until the last minute before gathering your belongings to get off a bus or train. This makes it more difficult for anyone to follow you.

If you feel threatened or unsafe on a bus or train, don't get off, as this may isolate you and put you in more danger. Instead, stay on the bus or train where there are other people.

Then get help from the other people around you, find the driver or guard, or hit the emergency bar.

When you get off a train or subway, you may have to use secluded stairwells, walkways, or paths to reach the exit. If possible, stay close to a mixed group of people. If you are alone and nervous about anybody loitering or following you, summon help or find a staff member. Don't worry about taking an extra 20 minutes to get home—it's better to stay safe.

dealing with suspicious bags

Keep an eye out for unattended bags. Although this problem is more often associated with airports, bags or packages left in bus and train

✔ AVOID SEXUAL MISCONDUCT

Attackers often deliberately choose rush hour to touch, grope, or expose themselves to someone on a subway, bus, or train, thinking that you will believe the incident was an accident or that you are unable to move. However, there are actions you can take:

☐ **Move away** If you can, move as far away as possible from the attacker. Even if he seems decent and apologizes, the safest action is to immediately move. Make sure that he is not following you.

☐ **Shout out** If you cannot move, or if he continues to harass you, then shout at him loudly to stop; this may embarrass him, and it certainly will get the attention of other passengers who can assist you.

☐ **Report flashers** If someone exposes himself to you, move away and attract the attention of the driver or those around you. Try to memorize a description of the culprit and report the incident as soon as possible.

Move away immediately if someone next to you on a train is touching you or rubbing up against you. Don't assume it is an accident.

stations are an equal threat and should be taken seriously. If you notice an abandoned bag, take responsibility and act quickly; don't hope that someone else will report it. If you are on a bus or train station, find a member of the staff or security who can follow established procedures. If you are in the street, call the police. Move away from the item, and don't use a cell phone to make the call, as the radio waves could set off an explosion.

call a cab

In many ways, taking a taxi is a very safe means of transportation. Unlike other forms of public transportation, there are no fellow passengers who could attack you, and you can be driven very close to your front door, which is particularly useful when coming home alone late at night. However, you should be careful about which cabs you choose.

plan ahead

If you're going out for an evening, take the phone number of a reputable cab company with you—if you don't know one, ask a friend. If you're worried about not having enough money at the end of the evening, put enough cash for your fare home in a separate wallet or pocket at the beginning of the evening.

order carefully

When you're out in a restaurant, bar, or other location, ask the staff for the number of a cab company, if you don't have one. If you are ordering the taxi yourself, be careful not to let anyone overhear when you give out your

personal information, such as your name and destination. It is possible that someone could go outside, pull up in his own car, and pretend to be your cab. Ask the cab company for the driver's name and the make and color of the car it is going to send. Don't give out too many details to the cab company, such as your house number—your first or last name, plus the street name, is sufficient.

check out the driver

Before you get into any cab, whether you've hailed it on the street or ordered it over the phone, a few basic checks can ensure your safety. Ask to see the driver's ID and radio before you get in. If you're suspicious, ask him to repeat the name and number of the cab company—if you have the company's number, you could always call it and confirm the registration and name of the driver. Always sit in the backseat of the cab, and if you talk to the driver, stick to general topics. Don't reveal any personal information, particularly if you live alone. Stay alert throughout the drive so that you can see where you are going. Carry a cell phone so you can call for help if you think that you are being driven the wrong way.

get keys ready

When you get close to home, have your money ready and have your keys in your hand or pocket. Ask to be dropped off a little distance from your front door, and if you're suspicious of the driver, wait for him to drive away before you go in.

Don't touch. Avoid the temptation to prod or poke an unattended parcel or bag. No matter how innocuous it may appear, there is the possibility that it contains an explosive. Get help from staff or the police.

safe travel abroad

Most people travel abroad without encountering any problems, and many areas of the world are considered just as safe as North America. However, unfamiliarity with an area or with local behavior can make you vulnerable, particularly if your guard is down because you are on vacation and feeling relaxed. But there is much you can do to avoid trouble and to minimize inconvenience if anything goes wrong.

do your research

The best way to stay safe in a foreign country is to find out as much as you can before traveling (see also page 152). You are less likely to become a target of crime if you understand the local culture and don't draw attention to yourself. Although travel companies can be useful, you need to look beyond what they provide. The Web sites of the U.S. Bureau of Consular Affairs (travel.state.gov) and the Government of Canada (www.passages.gc.ca) have up-to-date information about travel to any country in the world. You may also get help from the embassy for your country of travel— you can find its contact details in phone directories or on the Internet. Newspapers and TV are also good sources of updates on safety issues, political situations, unusual weather conditions, and possible terrorist activities.

obey the laws of the land

When you visit another country, you are subject to the laws of the country where you are staying. You do not have special protection because of your nationality. Make sure you find out about the laws and security regulations. Drug and weapon laws, for example, are often stricter abroad.

When you travel abroad, research before you go, and never assume that what is legal at home will be legal elsewhere.

Travelers have even been arrested for taking photographs of government buildings and airports or for purchasing antiques that are considered national treasures. If you do find yourself in trouble with the authorities, you must contact your closest embassy at once.

avoid trouble

Being in a vacation mood can sometimes make you lower your barriers. You may be more receptive to strangers and be less alert than you would be at home. This frequently makes tourists targets for criminals. To stay out of harm's way:

Learn about local customs to avoid causing offense. In some countries, men and women are expected to wear clothing that covers their shoulders and legs.

- **BE WARY OF STRANGERS** Be cautious of people who approach or try to befriend you, including children or people claiming to be tour guides—con artists come in many guises.
- **CARRY ID** Take your passport with you when you go out, as you will often be required to carry ID, but keep it in a secure internal pocket or a money belt inside your clothes. It is also a good idea to have photocopies of your passport and important documents, and keep them separately in your bag.
- **DON'T FIGHT BACK** Don't resist muggers or pickpockets unless there is a danger of being injured—you can usually claim property losses on your travel insurance. Don't carry anything you couldn't bear to lose.
- **TAKE CARE IN CROWDS** Be particularly alert in areas where you may be distracted, such as in markets, festivals, bars, and busy subways.

Here are some steps to take as you get ready for a trip abroad.

- ☐ **Be careful of cash** Take credit cards and traveler's checks instead of large amounts of cash. Record all their numbers and the phone numbers to call if you need to replace them. Keep this information separate from the cards and checks. Carry valuables in a concealed pocket or money belt rather than in a purse or fanny pack.

- ☐ **Check your insurance** Find out the level of health-care coverage your insurance provides. Canadian Medicare in some instances, for example, does cover you for trips abroad, whereas U.S. Medicare and Medicaid do not. If you're not covered for emergency medical treatment or flights home, consider supplemental insurance.

- ☐ **Leave a detailed itinerary** Tell your family or friends where to contact you in an emergency.

- ☐ **Leave your home documents in order** Check that copies of insurance policies and wills are accessible so that if anything does happen to you, your loved ones will be able to resolve matters easily.

- ☐ **Pack appropriate clothes** Wearing very expensive, trendy, or scruffy clothes can identify you as a tourist.

- ☐ **Take your medication** Pack enough medication to last the entire stay, and keep it in your hand luggage in case of baggage loss. Keep it in its original packaging to avoid security problems. If you need an unusual medication, carry a letter from your doctor explaining its purpose.

- ☐ **Travel light** Traveling with as few possessions as possible helps to keep from attracting attention. In addition, you will be able to move about from place to place more easily and more quickly.

stay somewhere safe

Plan your accommodations in advance if possible. If you arrive somewhere without a reservation, try the local tourist office, head for a reputable hotel chain, or use accommodation services found at airports and main stations, which should be regulated.

Book a hotel room between the second and seventh floors. These rooms are difficult for thieves to access, yet fire-fighting equipment can reach them easily.

The Overseas Security Advisory Council (see page 170) suggests that you request rooms away from elevators and stairwells, as these could be good hiding places for attackers.

When checking into your accommodations, take time to make sure that your room is secure, with adequate locks on the door and windows. Check for your nearest escape routes in case of fire, and count the number of doors you would have to pass to reach a stairwell—if there is thick smoke you won't be able to see clearly.

When you go out, leave your belongings in order so that you can see if anything has been disturbed, and conceal anything that may tempt an opportunist thief. Consider leaving valuables in a safe deposit box at reception. If possible, don't leave your room key or key card at the desk, as thieves may check the key board to see which rooms are unoccupied.

choose local rental cars

When choosing a car to rent, select a model that is common locally to avoid drawing attention to yourself. Make sure it bears no markings indicating it is a rental car. Check that the car works well before leaving the agency. Also, read your insurance documents carefully—confirm that there is a number you can call if you need emergency assistance. Make sure you have maps and have researched what the local traffic laws are. Abroad, as at home, follow all the guidelines for general car safety (see page 48).

women should keep alert

Lone female travelers may be considered easy targets for attack or robbery. But don't assume that every country is more dangerous than being at home. Even if women are expected to keep a low profile in the country they're visiting, it doesn't mean they will be more at risk; often, men in such countries will avoid them as long as they don't draw attention to themselves.

Keep your luggage within view or against your leg as you check into a hotel. If you are carrying a briefcase or purse, place it on the counter in front of you.

Read up on the local culture of the country you are visiting and how other female travelers have fared. In some places women are excluded from certain social activities or venues. Even if this custom irritates you, to go against the social norm is insulting and can even be dangerous.

Once you have arrived, be guided by how the local women dress, and cover up accordingly. Don't think that because other Western women are dressing in a certain way that it's appropriate; in some countries wearing shorts or sleeveless tops or leaving your head or face uncovered could bring unwanted attention. If you do get any crude comments, ignore them— don't encourage confrontation.

Don't go out on your own late at night, especially if you have been drinking, because this will make you less aware of your surroundings and more vulnerable. Instead, join other people, such as work colleagues or fellow travelers. If you need help, speak to your hotel's concierge or visit a local tourism office.

Never joke with staff or security officers that your luggage contains a bomb or weapon. They will react seriously, and you could miss your flight or be arrested.

stay safe in the skies

Millions of people travel by air every day, and it is still considered one of the safest methods of transportation. The U.S. National Safety Council says that it is 22 times safer to fly than to travel by car. Even with today's heightened security alerts, air travel is still trouble-free for most passengers. However, airlines understand that since the events of September 11, 2001, passengers have increased safety concerns, and air travel guidelines are under constant review.

pack your luggage yourself

You must pack your own bags and keep them with you at all times. Don't forget, too, that any gifts you may be carrying need to be unwrapped so that security officers can examine them, if necessary. Bear in mind other airport rules when packing. You will not be allowed on board carrying any kind of firearm, box cutter, or knife. Some cutting instruments, such as penknives or scissors, may also be prohibited from carry-on luggage. Contact your airline, the U.S. Transportation Security Administration (www.tsa.gov), or Transport Canada (www.tc.gc.ca) to get an updated list of items that are not allowed in the aircraft cabin.

STREETSMART

CHILD SAFETY Many airlines recommend using child seats for children weighing less than 40 lbs (20 kg). Remember to check with the airline to see if your child seat will fit onto the airline seat. Children weighing less than 20 lbs (10 kg) should be placed in a rear-facing child seat.

check safety procedures

No matter how many times you fly, always pay attention to the safety demonstration. The guidelines and equipment vary for every plane. Check whether there are life jackets or other flotation devices, and count the number of seats to your nearest emergency exit. This will help you react faster in an emergency when other people may be panicking and you may not be able to see clearly.

avoid turbulence injuries

The main cause of accidents during a flight is turbulence. Most injuries occur when passengers don't wear their seat belts, even when the seat belt sign is on. According to the U.S. Federal Aviation Administration, each year about 58 passengers in the United States are injured by air turbulence while not wearing their seat belts.

If you are feeling sleepy, make sure you buckle up before you doze off. If the seat belt sign goes on while you are asleep, crew members are instructed to wake you for your own safety.

prevent blood clots

The threat of deep vein thrombosis (DVT), or blood clots in the legs, is a concern for many travelers. While some cases have developed during short flights, the majority have been reported on long flights. Certain people are more at risk of deep vein thrombosis, including women taking contraceptive pills, pregnant women, and people with circulation problems. To help prevent DVT from occurring, take the following precautions:

- **DRESS COMFORTABLY** Wear loose-fitting clothing and consider special socks that provide gentle compression on affected areas.

Know how to fit a life jacket (right). It can save your life. In case of evacuation, remember that a life jacket should never be opened while inside the airplane.

Fasten your seat belt (opposite) whenever you are seated. Pilots may warn of turbulence ahead, but it is often unpredictable.

- **GET THE BLOOD FLOWING** Take a brisk stroll in the terminal while waiting for your flight. This will boost your circulation.
- **STRETCH YOUR LEGS** Stand up and walk around as much as you can during the flight.
- **EXERCISE IN YOUR SEAT** Wiggle your toes, move your ankles, and lift your legs up and down as much as you can when seated. Most in-flight magazines now include a simple in-chair exercise routine that you can follow.
- **DRINK PLENTY OF FLUIDS** Keep hydrated before, during, and after the flight. Avoid alcohol.

report drunkenness

Cramped conditions, low-cost flights, and alcohol have all led to an increased incidence of a behavior known as air rage. Because air rage is often fueled by alcohol, an airline can refuse to let people board if they appear to be under the influence of alcohol or drugs. If you see other passengers getting drunk or acting in a disorderly manner before you board the flight, bring it to the attention of airport staff. You could prevent not only trouble on board, but also delays in takeoff.

If another passenger becomes troublesome while on board, try to stay calm. If a passenger is aggressive toward you, try to reason with her first and defuse the situation. If this doesn't work, explain quietly to a crew member what the problem is and where the person is seated. Then return to your seat (or change seats), and let the crew member deal with the situation. All airline crews are trained in conflict management and have guidelines for dealing with troublesome passengers. As a last resort, they will use handcuffs and seat restraints.

defend yourself

Many people ask whether they should help if there is trouble on an airplane. Although the airlines would not advise passengers to get involved, certain situations may require it. If the trouble is verbal, allow the crew to do their job and to calm the party involved. However, if the incident escalates to physical threats or violence toward crew or passengers and you see no other alternative, then consider helping.

Don't forget, the law remains the same in the air as it does on the ground. Violence, assaults, and threats to life are criminal offenses and will be dealt with seriously upon landing.

In extreme situations, such as a terrorist attack, use your best judgment. It is impossible to give guidelines for all situations, but, in general, you should try to stay calm—your captors are likely to be nervous, so you don't want to antagonize them or draw attention to yourself. Comply with your hijackers' directions; defend yourself only as a last resort and use whatever means are necessary. If any shooting occurs, drop to the floor and keep your head down.

WHAT HAPPENS WHEN...

PASSENGERS GET INVOLVED
You have the same rights to defend your safety when in the sky as on the ground. In August 2000, Jonathan Burton broke through the cockpit door of a Boeing 737 jet, flying from Las Vegas to Salt Lake City. A number of passengers overpowered him, and during the violent struggle, Burton died of asphyxiation. A judge cleared the passengers of any wrongdoing on the grounds of self-defense.

stay safe on water

Many of us have a heightened sense of danger when we board a boat, possibly because of the proximity to water or because we feel insecure when moving. On top of specific boat safety issues, we also face the same threats as we do on land. No matter how long or short the journey, whether a vacation cruise or a hop across a river, remember that you have a responsibility to ensure your own and your family's safety; do not become complacent.

stay safe on cruise ships

The impressive cruise liners that tour today have the size and population of a small town. Safety and security are usually excellent, with well-planned procedures, but this does not mean that emergencies and crimes are unheard of.

To be prepared for incidents such as fires or sinking, read the safety advice in your cabin and pay attention to safety announcements. Attend the lifeboat drill, if available. Don't forget to establish with your family where evacuation points and lifeboats are located.

Remember that you are among strangers on a cruise ship, so petty theft or even personal attacks are possible. Observe the same caution as you would in a hotel room (see page 58), concealing your valuables and not opening your cabin door to strangers. Find out how to contact your steward in case of an emergency.

If an incident does happen, don't forget that you are protected by law. The laws that apply depend on whether you are within the jurisdiction of a nearby country or in international waters, where International Maritime Law will apply. Large companies will have on board security personnel who may detain the attacker until you dock, and most will have closed-circuit cameras to record evidence.

take care with cars on board

On ships or ferries that carry vehicles, one of the more hazardous areas you may be in is the car deck. When driving on board use patience and caution. Look out for pedestrians, who may be sharing a small area with you. Park your vehicle exactly where you are told to. The crew wants to ensure quick, safe, and even parking. Before you leave your car, make sure your parking brake is in place. Close and lock all windows and doors. Don't drink while on board if you will be driving the vehicle when you leave.

handling small boats

If you are on vacation, you may want to rent canoes, rowboats, or sailboats. You should always check weather information from a newspaper, radio, or TV forecast, or from a local Coast Guard bulletin board before you set out. Listen carefully to the operating instructions.

A "float plan" is a good way of letting people know your whereabouts in case an emergency occurs. Write down a detailed description of the boat, including all the passenger details, and, most important, your destination, time of departure, and time of return. Give the plan to a reliable friend who can alert the authorities if necessary. If you're delayed, contact those with your float plan to avoid an unnecessary search.

Check that there is a fire extinguisher on board, as well as oars if you are traveling in a motorboat. It is also advisable to have an anchor, a first aid kit, and distress flares if you are boating in large and open areas. To make sure you don't run out of gas, plan your trip to use one-third of gas on the outward journey, one-third for the return trip, and one-third to keep in reserve.

Remember to always secure and lock your boat when not on board. This includes while

Check the life jackets and make sure that there are enough for everyone before you set off. If not, ask the crew to provide more.

visiting marina restaurants or other piers. Never leave your boat accessible to others.

coping with an emergency

According to the U.S. Coast Guard, 70 percent of boating fatalities are due to capsizing, sinkings, and people falling overboard. If you do find yourself overboard and suddenly immersed in cold water, try not to panic. Try these hints:

- **CONSERVE ENERGY** Don't thrash about, as it will tire your muscles and cause you to waste energy you need to stay warm. Remove your shoes, but keep your clothes on.
- **KEEP YOUR HEAD ABOVE WATER** Concentrate on staying afloat and keeping your head dry— 50 percent of body heat loss is from the head. If your boat has capsized but is not in danger of sinking, get in or on top of the boat.
- **WAIT FOR HELP** Unless you can safely reach shore—which is usually farther away than it appears—wait with the boat until help arrives.

3

self-defense techniques

What would you do if somebody suddenly grabbed you by your clothes or around the neck? Prepare for your reaction, and learn the basic principles of defense. Find out how you can use everyday items as weapons, and practice escaping from 20 common holds by following the step-by-step diagrams.

the psychology of defense

If you act sensibly and plan ahead, the chances are that you will never be in a situation in which you have to physically defend yourself against an attacker. However, attacks really do happen, so it's worth taking the time to learn the techniques that will help you escape injury. This section looks at how to prepare yourself mentally now so that you won't hesitate to act if the worst should happen to you.

the right to defend yourself

Your safety, dignity, and well-being are precious. Nobody has the right to threaten, attack, or hurt you or to restrict your freedom. Should you be mugged in the street and your safety is in danger, it is important to realize that you do not have to be passive. You can fight back, using reasonable force (see below), to protect yourself from any harm and to escape.

know when to act

Some people are afraid that they might embarrass themselves by misjudging a situation. They worry, for example, about accusing somebody of following them only to find that they were mistaken. This fear of causing an awkward scene also can prevent someone from responding to bullying in the workplace (see page 46) or even dealing with domestic violence (see page 124). It is far better, however, to judge a situation wrongly and act to stay safe than to let someone attack you because you're too shy to say anything. It may be awkward, but you can always apologize if mistaken.

Some assailants rely on the fact that their victims will deny an attack is happening. A good example of this is when a man deliberately presses up against a woman on the subway. He is hoping that she will assume that it isn't his fault, and that she won't say anything or react negatively. An innocent man will do everything he can not to touch a woman on a train. So, if you ever find yourself in this situation, move or say something loudly; attracting attention often will be enough to embarrass your attacker and make him stop. If the man persists and the situation becomes more serious, you would have every right to hit back physically. It's up to you to judge what is right for your situation.

using reasonable force

Often, people worry about hurting an attacker while defending themselves, fearing that they may be arrested and charged themselves. When being attacked, you can't pause to think this or you will give your attacker the upper hand.

▮ STREETSMART

KNOW WHEN TO WALK AWAY Although your instincts may be correct in assessing when you are in a dangerous situation, be careful not to overreact to a problem. You can encounter aggressive behavior anywhere, and it can be frightening and threatening. However, don't automatically rise to provocation; instead, have the courage to walk or drive away.

Under most laws, individuals are allowed to defend themselves using "as much force as necessary." This phrase is somewhat vague because every situation is unique. Only you can decide what is necessary to defend yourself. However, to prevent people from abusing self-defense laws, certain parameters are taken into account. If called upon to justify your actions, you would have to convince others that you feared an immediate attack and had no alternative but to fight. Your defense also would have to be proportionate to the threat; if your life is not in danger, you can't threaten somebody else's life.

YOUR PERSONAL SPACE IS INVADED

Do you ever feel uncomfortable when somebody sits too close to you on a bus or shares your table in a coffee shop when there are others available? The anthropologist Edward T. Hall identified four personal space zones in which people interact: the intimate, personal, social, and public. However, "acceptable" behavior tends to vary among ages, sexes, and cultures. Therefore, if you think someone is invading your space, try to control any resentment you may feel. If it disturbs you, get up and move; your priority is always to avoid confrontation.

It can be hard to work out what is "reasonable" when you're scared and have to react quickly. The best advice is to do whatever feels right to defend yourself and expect a court to take this into account.

will fighting back make things worse?

Again, this depends on the situation you find yourself in. In some cases, you may feel that your best chance of survival comes from doing what the attacker asks. However, in other cases it may be better to fight back in order to create a possible getaway—you can never predict what an assailant has in mind.

protecting others

You are allowed to use "reasonable force" to defend others, such as people in your family or members of the public. However, you should not seek out someone threatening your family, as this is not self-defense—instead, contact the police for guidance and help.

Eye contact and distancing yourself physically, by holding up your hand, for example, can make you look confident and less vulnerable.

positive thinking

People of any age, build, or strength can learn
to defend themselves. This does not mean that
you will necessarily be able to overpower
someone who is bigger, but, even if you
consider yourself timid or nonviolent, you can
learn simple techniques that will give you the
time and space to escape.

It is important to acknowledge that an
attacker might be much stronger than you. Don't
take this negatively; if you train yourself to
think about this now, you're more likely to hit
an attacker as hard and as fast as you can to
enable you to get away from danger as soon as
possible. Women, in particular, are programmed
from an early age not to fight, but this does not
mean that they can't. Reading this book will
help you to prepare mentally and to show you
what you can do to protect yourself.

will I be any good at self-defense?

Many people who learn self-defense imagine
that they will find the techniques difficult or
unnatural, or that they will forget what to do
when the time comes. This is not the case.

**Anyone, whether of an aggressive nature or not,
can inflict great pain on an attacker.**

Taking time to practice the moves on the
following pages will help you get over your
initial fears and gain vital self-confidence. All of
the techniques are easy to use, and once you
master them, they will stay in your mind in case
you need to use them. You might not react
exactly like the illustrations, or you may forget
some things, but this does not matter—the
important factor is that you will have learned to
do whatever you need to do to defend yourself
and escape from a threatening situation.

understand your reaction

Everyone reacts differently to a dangerous
situation: Mental shock can make you feel
unsteady and confused, and you also may suffer
physical symptoms, such as an inability to move
(see page 15). Alternatively, you may feel calm
and distanced from the event. These are natural
reactions, and whichever one you experience,
remember you do have the strength and courage
to fight back.

overcome distaste

The instinct to survive and get away can help
you overcome emotional responses to an attack,
such as squeamishness. However, it can be a
good idea to take time now to prepare for
emotions you might experience and actions you
might have to take. If, for example, you're
fighting at close quarters and your attacker is

Simple techniques (opposite), such as bending back your attacker's little finger, are very effective and require little strength or skill.

People of all abilities (left) and ages can learn techniques that will help protect them from an attacker.

drunk or unclean, it is important that you are ready to ignore any feelings of disgust—you may need to scratch or bite him to break free. You also may have to do something that you would never do in normal life, such as poke someone's eyes (see page 96) or grab an attacker's testicles (see page 101).

timing is crucial

An attacker has the advantage of surprise over you. He will not be expecting you to know what is going on and will count on you being scared. The quicker you gather your thoughts, the faster you can defend yourself. Your attacker might not have considered his next move, so the sooner you fight back, the better. If you wait to react, you might find yourself growing weaker, as the adrenaline surge turns to tiredness. So fight back right away.

WHAT HAPPENS WHEN...

YOU'RE AFRAID

Although the surge of adrenaline you experience when you're frightened can give you additional strength and speed to fight off an attacker (see page 14), it also causes you to lose your finer motor skills—the ability to move your muscles in a precise way. For example, when you're sitting down and relaxed, it's relatively easy to thread a needle. However, if you try it after running around the block, thus increasing your adrenaline levels, you won't be able to perform this intricate action. This is why the self-defense techniques in this book involve simple movements. If you practice them repeatedly, you'll be able to perform them without thinking.

fighting back

The self-defense techniques in this chapter are grouped according to the body area where you may be attacked and whether that attack comes from the front or from behind. Of course, a real attack may not happen exactly as illustrated, but the moves shown here are designed to be both memorable and effective in most circumstances.

the power of practice

To give yourself the best protection, you need to practice self-defense techniques regularly. You will get the most out of them if you learn them with somebody you trust—somebody who will take the exercise seriously. In that way you'll be helping your friend learn life-saving skills too. When practicing make sure you have plenty of room to maneuver and wear loose-fitting clothes and flat shoes. Follow each sequence of movements slowly, going through the motions without actually making contact when you hit or kick. As you get used to the motions, build up your speed. Be careful not to hit your partner at full thrust to avoid causing pain. If you want to know what it feels like to hit something, punch a cushion or mattress.

make a difference

You can increase your self-confidence and ability to deal with a potentially frightening situation very easily:

- Check your anger levels. Think about how you respond to and deal with other people. If you're quick to anger, take a few moments to breathe deeply before you speak.

- Learn self-defense techniques. Nobody expects you to be an expert in minutes or even days, but practicing just a few simple moves can give you the confidence to defend and protect yourself from an attacker.

- Pay more attention to your everyday movements. For example, when you walk down the street, tread confidently and remain alert at all times.

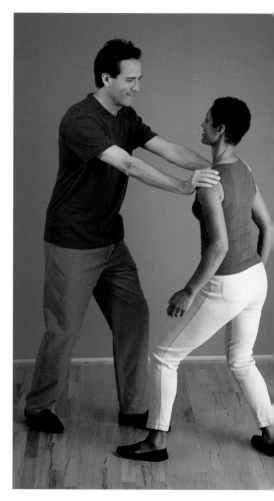

Balance is a key part of self-defense (see page 73). Practice with a friend to get the best results.

group attacks

Although these are among the least common types of attacks, they can be the most frightening. Groups are particularly dangerous because the pack instinct comes into play. Members egg each other on to commit greater acts of violence than they might do alone. There are, however, steps you can take to protect yourself. As most martial arts experts will tell you, only fight back against a group of attackers if you have no other choice; your first priority is to run away. If you can't see an escape route, try the following.

talk your way out

One of the best things to do in this circumstance is to attempt to talk your way out. Calm the situation by being calm yourself. Try to appear as nonaggressive as possible by standing with open arms and hands rather than clenched fists. Tell the group in a steady voice that you do not want to fight any of them.

stay on your feet

No matter what happens, your priority is to stay on your feet. If you fall to the floor, you leave yourself open to attack. Back up against a car or a wall to protect yourself from attack from behind, and make use of the balance techniques described on page 73.

look for the leader

Turn your attention to the biggest or loudest person in the group or anyone with a weapon. Speak to that person with confidence. If you can't reason with him and have to fight, aim your defensive techniques at that person first. If you manage to fight off the most threatening attacker, the others may hesitate, giving you a chance to run to safety.

PRACTICE YOUR AIM

No matter how big or strong an attacker is, he has vulnerable parts of the body, as outlined below. Keep these areas in mind when you look at the defense options later in this chapter. Of course, these body parts are also areas you should protect.

- ☐ **Hair** Grabbing a handful and pulling causes pain, giving you control of somebody's head.

- ☐ **Eyes** Poking or gouging your attacker in the eyes can cause temporary or even permanent blindness, giving you a good chance of escape. Only use this in serious attacks.

- ☐ **Ears** Slapping, punching, or biting the ears can be painful and cause damage, as the ears contain hundreds of little bones and are attached only by flaps of skin.

- ☐ **Nose** Striking or biting the nose is easy, because it protrudes, and can cause your attacker's eyes to water, giving you a chance to escape.

- ☐ **Neck and throat** Punching the throat can be very painful but can also cause severe damage. Only aim here in a serious situation.

- ☐ **Breastbone** Striking the front of the chest can cause a surprising amount of pain.

- ☐ **Stomach** Punching or kicking the stomach can wind your attacker.

- ☐ **Groin** Punching or striking here will hurt someone of either sex but will be extremely painful to a man—enough to incapacitate him while you escape. Kneeing in the groin is difficult but very effective (see page 80).

- ☐ **Thighs** Kneeing the thigh is agonizing and can temporarily prevent your attacker from putting weight on the affected leg.

- ☐ **Knees and shins** Kicking this area is painful and can cause a distraction to let you escape.

- ☐ **Ankles and feet** Stamping on the feet or ankles can be very painful, particularly if wearing high or solid heels.

six steps to safety

The basic principles of defense are the same, whatever your situation. You want to get away from your attacker quickly and with as few injuries as possible. To achieve this, there are six steps you should bear in mind.

1 attract attention

The first line of defense you have is to scream or shout at the top of your lungs and straight in your attacker's face. During a struggle it can deter your attacker in a number of ways. Not only will it be unexpected, but criminals won't want people to come to your aid or act as witnesses, so shouting can be enough to scare your attacker away. If you injure your attacker in a struggle, witnesses will be able to state what you were shouting, proving you to be the victim and not the aggressor. Also, an attacker will have to concentrate on keeping you quiet—which could be enough of a distraction to allow you to escape.

For you, the screaming or shouting is literally a moment to catch your breath. Before or after you scream, you will naturally take a deep breath, pulling in oxygen to help your brain function and fuel your muscles to fight. Psychologically, shouting empowers you; it is a positive action and prepares you for the next step.

As with all self-defense techniques, remember that practice makes perfect. The shock and terror of an attack can cause you to freeze, which is why it's important to practice screaming and shouting at home until these become instinctive reactions. Ask a friend to grab you from behind and try screaming at the top of your lungs. Make sure it comes from your lungs and not just your throat. It may feel strange, but it's important to try—when was the last time you really screamed your loudest?

✔ BE READY TO SHOUT

Shouting out a command can make you feel more in control and sound more assertive. Avoid submissive reactions, such as "help me" or "please let go," as they will make your attacker think that you are scared. Try one of these instead:

☐ **"Get back!"**

☐ **"Let go!"**

☐ **"Go away!"**

☐ **"Stop it!"**

☐ **"Police!"**

☐ **"Get off!"**

☐ **"Fire!"**

2 stay in the open

One of your priorities if you do get attacked is to stay in an open, public place, if at all possible. Don't let your attacker force you to a second location, such as a car, alley, or house. Something worse may be awaiting you there, and you will have less chance of attracting help. Do anything you can to prevent being dragged away—struggle furiously or grab hold of a railing or lamppost. If you have no other option, try dropping to the ground like a dead weight (see page 108)—although you should usually try to stay on your feet, somebody may come to your aid while you are struggling on the ground. For defense techniques you can use in such a situation, see page 110.

3 keep your balance

If you are to avoid being knocked to the ground—a very vulnerable position—and if you want to be able to run away at your first chance, it can help to know how to maintain your balance. Often this is the first thing taught in self-defense classes. When struggling up close, it will be easier to stay on your feet if you grab your attacker or his clothing—if you are knocked to the ground, you are likely to also take him down with you. An attacker may not want to risk this, because it will put him in a vulnerable position.

Practice your balance with a friend. Ask her to push and pull you by the shoulders to see if you are steady. Strengthen your stance by placing your legs about shoulder-width apart, with one foot in front and one just behind you. Bend your knees slightly, like shock absorbers. Now, quickly swivel your hips from side to side. If you are steady on your feet, you have good balance. If you are falling in any direction, you do not. Bend your knees a little more or move your feet wider or closer together. Remember: Practice makes perfect.

4 make your escape

Your ultimate goal whenever you are being attacked is to escape safely. This means not only doing everything you can to fight off your attacker and prevent injury to yourself, but also being sure not to fight longer than necessary. As soon as you see a chance to run for it, take it. Don't continue hitting or kicking your attacker. It may give him a chance to attack you again, since you will have lost the element of surprise and he will be more prepared. Also, the police could consider unnecessary and continued fighting as a revenge attack from you. Once you've broken free, watch where you're going—you don't want to trip over an obstacle or run into the road.

5 decide whether to fight

If you can't get help or escape your attacker, you will then have to choose whether to fight or not. No one else can make that decision for you, and it depends entirely on your situation. You probably won't know how you'll react until something happens. In principle, however, remember that property always can be replaced, but your life can't. If somebody grabs your handbag in the street, it may be best just to let it go. Also, if somebody is threatening you or a loved one with a weapon, it's best to do exactly as he says. Nobody would blame you, nor should you blame yourself, if you don't put up a struggle.

If you do decide to fight because you feel you would be injured further or even killed if you didn't, then you should put 100 percent effort into it. It's no good fighting halfheartedly—your blows will be weak. Having a positive mental attitude will mean that every scream, punch, or kick is forceful and brings you one step closer to escape.

6 seek help

If you've been attacked, report it to the police as soon as possible. Don't go home or wait until a cop comes past, but get to a safe place right away and use your cell phone or a pay phone, on which the call will be free. If there is a store, bar, or gas station nearby, go inside—the door will be unlocked, so you'll be able to get in immediately. Also, there will be staff and customers there to help you and be witnesses. Wait there until the police arrive. If you are on a residential street, and there is nowhere public to go, don't be afraid to knock on someone's door and ask to use the phone. Although the people in the house may be strangers, the risks that they may harm you are far less than if you stay on the street with your attacker. Wait inside for the police to arrive.

using weapons

When confronted by an attacker, use whatever means you can to escape. This includes using whatever you have on hand to fight him off. Your purse, umbrella, or a rock on the ground can make an effective weapon, especially if your attacker is stronger than you.

carrying a weapon

If your life is in danger, your first concern is to defend yourself. This does not mean, however, that you should carry an illegal weapon. In some states, provinces, and countries, this would include a flick knife, sharpened metal object, or a piece of martial arts equipment. If you do carry any of these, you risk being arrested—even if you only use it in self-defense. Household items, such as kitchen knives, hammers, or screwdrivers, also should not be carried. Unless you can prove that you needed the item that day for work, the law will treat you as if you were carrying an offensive weapon. The law varies among countries, states, and provinces as to what kind of weapon, if any, an individual may carry. For the most up-to-date information, consult your local police department.

Even if you consider carrying a legally owned weapon, it's worth noting that in most attacks, a gun or a can of pepper spray would be completely useless. It's very unlikely that you would be able to get one of these weapons out of your briefcase or bag in time, and there is a chance that you might injure yourself while trying to use it against your attacker. This is why the following pages describe how to defend yourself using everyday items that you may have in your hand, such as an umbrella or cell phone, as well as self-defense techniques that require nothing but your hands, feet, or other parts of your body.

guns: are they safe?

This is a highly charged, emotional issue, with strong arguments made for both sides of the

Improvised weapons can be made out of everyday objects such as a handbag or a folded umbrella.

Household weapons like those generally found in the kitchen or toolbox, may be classified as illegal if carried on you or used in an encounter.

case. Organizations such as the U.S.-based Brady Center to Prevent Gun Violence, named after Jim Brady, press secretary to President Reagan, who was shot during the 1981 assassination attempt, are highly visible in their campaign to restrict gun use, while other groups produce statistics to show that legal gun ownership does not lead to an increased risk of violence, including homicide.

According to the U.S. National Crime Prevention Council (NCPC), a gun in the home increases the risk of homicide three times and the risk of suicide five times. The NCPC suggests that for self-protection purposes you might consider other home security measures first, such as purchasing an alarm system or a dog. However, if you do choose to keep a gun, make sure that you do the following:

- **UNLOAD** Always take the ammunition out.
- **LOCK IT UP** Keep it in a secure locked case or cupboard, preferably hidden from children.
- **STORE KEYS SEPARATELY** Don't keep the keys and ammunition in the same place as you keep household keys.

Although these precautions might seem like common sense, the U.S.-based KidsHealth organization (www.kidshealth.org) reports that 39 percent of people who own guns don't lock them up. Also, keep cleaning supplies locked away, as these products are often poisonous.

Bear in mind that the laws on gun ownership vary in every country, state, and province. For up-to-date information, consult your local police department. This is important if you are traveling between the United States and Canada or between different states. You should also consult your local police department for license and registration guidance. You may need to attend a safety training program, provide fingerprints, produce a clean record, prove you have no history of mental illness, and pay a fee. In Canada you can obtain information about gun laws by calling 1-800-731-4000 or by visiting www.canadianfirearms.com.

common defensive objects

If you are attacked while out on the street, there are several items, which you may be carrying in your hand, pocket, or bag, that you can use to defend yourself. Many hard objects, such as a cell phone, can be used to hit an attacker, while keys can slash your attacker's face and aerosol sprays can be aimed at your attacker's eyes.

Keys make powerful weapons to stab at or slash across your attacker's eyes and face. Hold the key ring in your fist, with one key grasped, point outward, between your thumb and forefinger. Don't hold the key between your fingers, as it will cut you badly if you punch with it.

Bags, briefcases, and purses can be flung into your attacker's knees, crotch, or head. Before you hit with a bag, make sure you have a good grip on the handle. If you swing quickly and with force, you can also use a bag to knock a weapon out of somebody's hand.

Aerosol sprays, such as perfumes, antiperspirants, or hairsprays, can be directed into an attacker's eyes or used to hit him in a sensitive area, such as the face or chest. Hold the bottle tightly with the nozzle facing forward and your thumb on top.

Pens or pencils are good defensive weapons as they are easily concealed. Hold the pen or pencil in the palm of your hand, point downward, and clasp your fingers around it. Put your thumb on top of it to stop it from sliding as you strike. Use a stabbing motion.

Umbrellas, if they are strong and folded, can be used like a bat to hit vulnerable areas on an attacker. Hold the umbrella toward the middle and take a quick swing before you hit. Aim for the crotch, head, ribs, neck, or any other sensitive area.

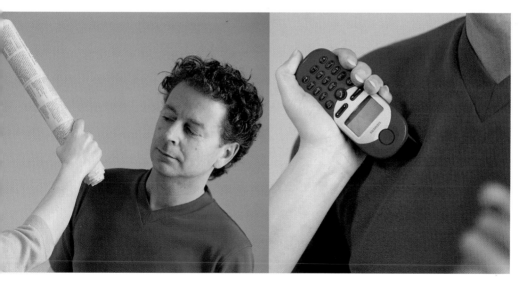

Newspapers, if rolled up, can make sturdy defensive weapons if you're attacked. Use a sideways stabbing motion to hit an assailant in the temple, or swing the newspaper hard into a sensitive area, such as the neck, chest or crotch.

Cell phones can be used as weapons. Wrap your fingers around your cell phone with your thumb on the end. Use a downward, stabbing motion into a sensitive part of the body. If there is an antenna, use that to stab your attacker.

wrist grips

These techniques will enable you to escape if someone grabs your wrist or wrists. This is a very common way of restraining someone, and it can be used in playfulness or in anger. However, if the person won't let go, it can be intimidating; you've been denied your freedom to leave, and you have the right to stop it. The person grabbing you probably doesn't mean you any harm; if you're a woman being held by a man, he may not realize his own strength or understand that it will worry you. Simply telling him in a firm tone to "let go" may well do the trick. If he doesn't, however, it's time to act. Use the element of surprise to your advantage.

single wrist grip

This is probably the most common assault you will face. It can happen quickly during an argument if you try to walk away, but the person you are arguing with wants to stop you.

1 **EXERT YOUR STRENGTH** Turn to face your attacker, look him in the eyes to show that you are serious and not scared, and order him to "let go." If he refuses, make a fist with the hand that he is holding. This will make your wrist feel stronger and ready to pull away.

try this...

STAMPING AND KICKING Don't be afraid to kick or stamp when trying to get away from an attacker. Find your balance by bending your knees slightly. Look down to where you want to aim. If you are standing close, you could grab onto your assailant's clothing or pinch the skin on his arms to support yourself and to help you keep your balance.

Moving quickly, stamp hard on the front of the ankles. Alternatively, use short, fast movements to kick your attacker's shins, ankles, or kneecaps. Turn your toes upward and kick hard with the sole of your foot—it's safer and more effective than kicking with your toes. Aiming low will allow you to move faster and will keep your legs out of his reach so that he cannot grab them. Keep kicking until he lets go of you, giving you the chance to escape.

3 USE THE WEAK SPOT Your attacker's hand is weakest where his thumb is on your wrist, so pull hard and fast sideways or upward against his thumb to break free. This is much more effective than twisting in his grip. Take a step backward as you do so—your legs will give you extra power.

2 USE YOUR OTHER HAND If you don't have the strength in one hand, prepare to use two. Grab your trapped fist with your free hand ready to pull free.

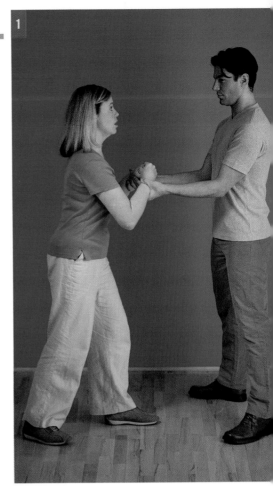

double wrist grip

An attacker who takes hold of both your wrists does so believing that he will have control of your hands and therefore the rest of you. However, if somebody has hold of both of your hands, it means that he is more open to a defensive move from you. If you can find your balance, you can knee or kick your assailant as a distraction while you try to free your wrists. If you can free your stronger arm, you will be able to fight with that hand.

1 FIND YOUR BALANCE Bend your knees and elbows slightly. Brace yourself so that you offer better balance and resistance to your attacker and can stop him from pulling you around. Clench both fists to make your arms feel stronger and order him to "let go."

try this...

KNEE DEFENSE Your knee can deliver a powerful blow to an attacker. However, the knee's range is limited and is effective only when you are struggling up close.

First, find your balance. Move quickly to give yourself more chance of staying upright, and pull your opponent toward you and down onto your knee as you move it upward. Aim for anywhere on the thighs or groin, whatever the sex of your attacker. A hit to the outer thighs can cause great pain, which may be enough to prevent your attacker from chasing you.

tactical tips

- Try to free your stronger hand first. You have more chance of success, and if it is your right hand, it probably will be held by your attacker's left hand, which is usually the weaker one.

- If you manage to release one hand, you can use it to help free your other trapped hand.

- Keep kicking your attacker's legs as a distraction. He won't want to hold on to somebody who is thrashing about and causing him pain. Also, if you connect, he may not be able to pursue you when you escape.

- Remember that he will not be able to defend himself from your kicks or knees unless he lets go of your wrists, which will then be your chance to break free.

2 CREATE A DISTRACTION Kick your attacker in the legs and keep kicking until he lets go or until you can see a chance to wrench your arms free. Kick with your toes turned upward to protect them.

3 FREE YOUR WRISTS As in the single wrist grip, don't pull toward you, but pull upward or sideways against your attacker's thumbs as quickly as you can. Put strength into it and really mean what you are doing.

clothes-grabbing

Many fights, particularly between men, start by one person grabbing the front of the other's clothes. Often a fight stems from an argument in which an attacker wants to dominate you physically, perhaps because he has failed to do so mentally. An attacker may also want to grab your clothes to restrain you if you are trying to walk or run away.

Initially, it may seem that this is a less aggressive move than some others, because your attacker is holding your clothing and not your body. However, you should be wary as it means that the other person is not afraid of you and thinks you are weaker than him. Your attacker may be holding you in preparation for a punch

or a head butt. Whatever the thinking behind it, you are being denied your freedom to leave, and you have a right to free yourself, even if that means hurting your attacker.

one-handed lapel grip

If your attacker grabs your clothes in one hand, he is left with a free hand, which he can use to follow up with a punch while he holds you in position. Show your strength by acting quickly. If you scream in his face, this may be enough to cause your attacker to panic and run away. Your scream will also act like a battle cry before you remove your attacker's hand forcefully and make your escape.

1 **PULL BACK** Keep your head and shoulders away from your attacker's head. This will enable you to watch his free hand and prevent him from head-butting or biting you anywhere. Moving away will also show your resistance. Put your hands up near your face, ready to fend off a punch.

try this...

KICK TO THE BODY If you have managed to twist your attacker's hand but cannot break free, he will still be in an open and vulnerable position. If he is leaning forward, try a kick to his ribs or stomach, pulling your attacker toward your kick. A kick to the ribs will be extremely painful, while a kick to the stomach will wind him, leaving him unable to get up and chase you. When you kick in this way, use the top of your foot, as if you were kicking a ball dropped down onto it. Don't try this if your attacker is upright and composed as he could grab your raised leg as you kick.

3 ESCAPE Once you've ripped your attacker's hand off your clothing, use your free hand to push down on his upturned elbow. Bending the elbow in the wrong direction can cause severe pain, so this elbow lock should force your opponent to the floor, allowing you to make your escape.

2 GRIP AND TWIST Turn to face your opponent. Grab hold of the hand that is holding you, using your same hand—if he is holding you with his right hand, take hold of him with your right hand and the same with the left. Put your four fingers over the top of his hand and grip under the edge of the hand, near his little finger. Then twist his hand down toward the thumb. This will force his elbow up and cause him to let go. It will also tilt his head down, knocking him off balance (see page 95).

two-handed lapel grip

An attacker who grabs your clothing by two hands is trying to demonstrate his superior strength to you. He is informing you that he means business and wants to control the situation and you. The longer you allow the other person to do this, the more confident he will become, so you must act quickly to demonstrate that you are not afraid to fight back, if necessary.

1 STEADY YOURSELF Don't make it easy for the other person to pull you around. Move your legs about shoulder-width apart and bend your knees slightly to give yourself more balance. Take hold of your attacker's arms or clothing and pull him toward you a little; this will put him off-balance and give you the advantage.

try this...

TWO-HANDED EAR STRIKE If your hands are free and you are able to reach, consider striking your attacker's ears. This can momentarily deafen and confuse your opponent and cause him great pain.

To strike, keep your elbows bent slightly, and swing both arms simultaneously and quickly toward the ears. Aim to strike with your hands at around a 60-degree angle, and make sure that your hands are slightly cupped, since this will have more effect. When you make contact, you also may hit the jawbone and the temple, nerve centers that are very close to the brain and so cause acute pain. However, if this move doesn't work the first time, don't repeat it, as your attacker will be prepared and lean his head away.

2 **MAKE YOUR ATTACKER LET GO** Still holding your attacker's arms, start kicking his kneecaps, shins, or ankles. Look down to where you want to aim your kicks, and kick hard and fast. Turn your toes up to protect them. You should cause enough pain to make him let go and allow you to escape.

one-handed grab from behind

If someone seizes your clothes from behind, your natural instinct will be to keep moving forward. This is a good thing to do, as it can stop you from being taken somewhere that you don't want to go, and it may give you the few extra seconds you need to attract attention. However, if your attacker won't let go, employ the technique below to force him to release his hold and allow you to escape.

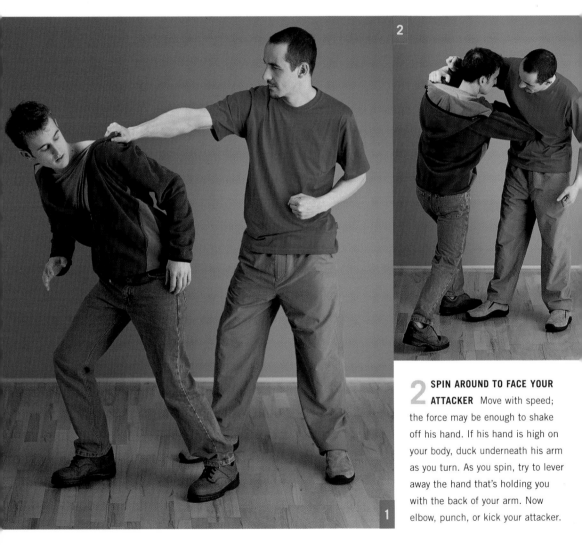

2 SPIN AROUND TO FACE YOUR ATTACKER Move with speed; the force may be enough to shake off his hand. If his hand is high on your body, duck underneath his arm as you turn. As you spin, try to lever away the hand that's holding you with the back of your arm. Now elbow, punch, or kick your attacker.

1 TENSE YOUR BODY, READY FOR ACTION Lean slightly forward, away from your attacker's grip. Your clothes will be stretched, but it will give you vital time to think and space to maneuver.

two-handed grab from behind

This is harder to escape from as your attacker will have a better grip. Although it may be your instinct to pull away, it's better to spin around and face your attacker in order to break free.

PALM STRIKE The chin and nose are very sensitive areas of the face, which, when hit, can make the eyes water and sting. A hard hit to either will confuse your attacker and leave him reeling. When you strike, you should smash upward, hard and fast, forcing his head back and away from you. Use the bony lower part of the palm, and keep your fingers slightly curled so that you'll be ready to scratch his face, if required.

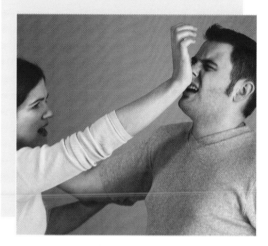

1 LEAN FORWARD Find your balance by widening your stance and bending your knees slightly. Lean away from your attacker, but look around to see what his hands are doing.

2 SPIN AROUND Raise your elbows toward your chest. Spin quickly to face your attacker. If you keep your elbows tense and move quickly, you should be able to knock your attacker's hands away. You may even knock your attacker off balance and be able to push him to the ground.

hair-pulling

Almost anyone can assault you in this way, since it doesn't require much strength. Hair-pulling is commonly used by children fighting in the playground or by women fighting each other. Hair-pulling is very painful and takes control of your head, which, in turn, can make it difficult for you to keep upright. The following techniques show you what to do if someone grabs you from the front or behind, either with one hand or two.

one-handed hair pull

This type of attack may occur if you are arguing with someone face to face. When somebody pulls your hair at the front of your head, it can be very painful, because this is the most tender part of your scalp. It also pulls your head down, so you can't see what's coming next, making you feel very vulnerable. However, there are ways that you can ease the pain and make your escape.

1 KEEP YOUR BALANCE You are better able to defend yourself if you can stay on your feet. Position your legs so that they are about shoulder-width apart, with one slightly behind the other. Shout at her to "stop and let go."

tactical tips

- A strong knee to the groin or thigh is effective. You don't have to hit between the legs—anywhere will cause pain.

- Don't panic if you can't stand up straight. Kick toward the ankles and shins to escape.

- If you use a hand strike, use your top hand, even if this isn't your strongest hand, as you must leave one hand in place to stop any hair-pulling.

try this...

KNIFE HAND TO THE GROIN If you flatten out your hand with your thumb held in close to the side, you can make a small but hard-hitting weapon, which can fit into narrow spaces. The knife hand is ideal for hitting somebody in the groin because it will fit through a smaller gap than a knee, foot, or fist. Also, if you initially strike the inside of the thigh, your hand will be slim enough to be guided up into the groin area. To use this technique, begin with your hand by your thigh, then bring it upward between the legs in a sharp, chopping movement. The effect will be very painful for a woman and agonizing for a man.

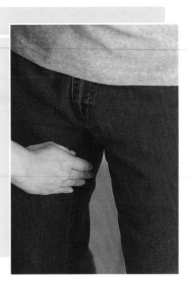

3 DEFEND YOURSELF Keeping your hands on hers, stand up as straight as you can. Since your attacker is up close to you, a knee to her groin should be enough to make her stop. Look for your target area before you strike and try to make the first hit count.

2 EASE THE PAIN Put both your hands on top of the hand your attacker is using to pull your hair, and push down. This will prevent your hair from being pulled, and the pain will ease almost immediately, allowing you to think more clearly.

two-handed hair pull

This is twice as strong and twice as painful as the one-handed hair pull. Putting your hands on top of your attacker's and pushing down will help ease the pain, but with four hands pushing on your head, there will be a lot of pressure on your neck and shoulders. This may not trouble you at the time, because your adrenaline will be pumping, but later you may find that your neck and shoulders are stiff and painful. The advantage of this technique is that both of your attacker's hands will be occupied, giving you more freedom to defend yourself. If at any stage you remove one of your hands to strike and it becomes too painful, just put it back again and use kneeing and kicking techniques.

1 **PREPARE YOURSELF** Start shouting to attract help, and widen your legs to help your balance. Stop the pain as soon as possible by putting both of your hands on top of your attacker's and pressing down onto your head. This will show that you are prepared to resist. To prevent your attacker from pushing your head down and kneeing you, stand upright and as far back as you can, away from your attacker's hands and legs.

2 **TWIST AND SIDE KICK** If your attacker is holding you at arm's length, get closer by turning yourself toward her. As you twist, keep a tight grip on her hands. This will force her wrist in the wrong direction, causing pain and knocking her off balance. Lift the leg nearest to her about 1 ft. (30 cm) off the ground and kick out to the side with the edge and heel of your foot, aiming for her shin or ankle. Don't lift your leg too high, or you could lose your balance. Lift your hands slightly to enable her to remove her hands from your head.

try this...

PUNCH TO THE FACE If you are able to stand up straight and use one of your hands, a punch to the face can be very effective. However, for your own safety, you should practice punching before you try it in a real situation. Use a punching bag at the gym, or try hitting something soft, such as a cushion.

When you make a fist, keep your thumb on the outside of your fingers. Don't bend your wrist, but keep it strong, with your hand in a straight line with your arm. Move from the shoulder for maximum power, and bend your elbow slightly. Aim for a point beyond where you are going to hit, as if you were hitting through your attacker. Don't take a big swing, as your assailant may see it coming and turn away. Screaming as you punch also can add aggression to the strike.

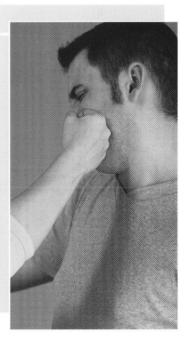

hair pull from behind

The surprise and discomfort of being grabbed from behind can put you in a vulnerable position. Having your hair in a ponytail can make it easier for an attacker, but she also can get a good hold of short hair by grasping you at the top of your head. To keep control, your attacker will grab as much hair as possible and twist or pull it very tightly. She may feel more confident of staying anonymous if attacking you from behind, so your attacker will be surprised when you turn around.

1 GRAB YOUR ATTACKER'S HAND Take a deep breath, scream, and shout. Try to keep your balance by planting your feet firmly. Grab your attacker's fist with both of your hands and press down onto your head as hard as you can.

2 FACE YOUR ATTACKER Keep hold of your attacker's hand and twist your whole body around to face her. Keep your wrists tense, as this will push your attacker's wrist into an awkward position. Place your legs about shoulder-width apart, with your knees slightly bent for better balance.

try this...

PUNCH TO THE GROIN Although your legs can exert more force on an area, your hands can move up to five times faster. Also, hands are more maneuverable, so if you can't get your leg into the space between you and your attacker, or if you are worried about falling over, use your fist to hit him in the groin area. Try to look at where you are aiming. Turn your head if your attacker is behind you. If you are bending forward, it may be easier to punch downward. Make a fist with your hand, keeping the thumb outside of the fingers, then punch sharply into the groin. Don't jab and pull back; punch as if you want to smash right through your assailant into the ground.

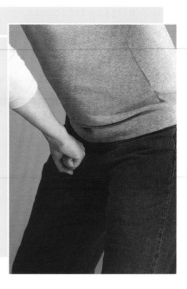

3 DEFEND YOURSELF Now facing your attacker, use your knees, feet, or hands to defend yourself until you can escape. Keeping your thumb outside of your fingers, punch sharply into the ribs, or if your attacker's legs are apart, knee her in the groin area, using as much force as necessary.

attacks to the neck

The throat is a very vulnerable part of the body, containing the windpipe and the arteries that supply blood to the brain. No matter how strong you are, if somebody grips and puts pressure on your throat, it is a painful and life-threatening situation. Even one hand squeezing your throat may cut off the blood supply to the brain and cause you to lose consciousness in as little as four seconds, leaving you helpless in the hands of an attacker. Attacks to the neck are often committed by men on women, as the attacker needs to be much stronger than his victim to prevent a struggle. The fear for women is that such a hold may be the precursor to sexual assault. Whenever someone holds you in this

way, know that he means business and is willing to hurt you seriously. For all of these reasons, you must remove that hand very quickly. The following techniques require little strength yet are highly effective. If you practice them with a friend, they will become instinctive, giving you vital seconds to protect yourself.

one-handed throat grip

Even if you are only being held by one hand, this is a serious situation. You should try not to panic and aim to make your first escape attempt count. While watching out for your attacker's free hand, you must try to remove the clamped hand as quickly as possible.

Make your neck strong. With any type of attack to the neck, you can provide some protection for your arteries, veins, and windpipe by strengthening your neck. Practice this by clenching your jaw, tucking your chin down into your neck, and slightly hunching both your shoulders.

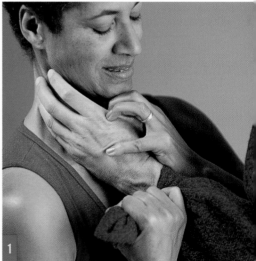

1 GRIP HIS HAND With one hand, grab your attacker's hand, if possible between his thumb and your neck, where there will be a space. With your other hand, grip firmly his wrist or sleeve.

try this...

ARM LOCK If at any stage in a struggle you have managed to grab hold of your attacker's hand, you can try an arm lock to force him to the ground. Grab your attacker's hand with your same hand: If he is using his right hand, hold his hand with your right hand; if he is using his left, take hold with your left (see page 83). Twist his arm so that his elbow is pointing upward. Now using your free arm, smash down hard on his upturned elbow with your elbow. This will then throw him off balance and can even be enough to break his arm, if necessary.

tactical tips

- Kick an attacker in the legs as you reach to take his hand off your throat. This may be enough of a distraction to allow you to rip the hand away.

- Any damage you've sustained from a throat grab might prevent you from screaming or shouting, even after the attacker has let go. This is when a whistle or rape alarm is useful.

- If you can't get an attacker's hand off, use your other hand to strike him on the nose or chin with a palm strike (see page 87).

- Once you have removed your attacker's hand from your throat, stop him from grabbing you there again. Watch his hands and keep your chin slightly down until you can break free.

2 REMOVE HIS HAND Using as much force as possible, rip his arm down and away from you. At the same time, pull your head and shoulders back away from him. If this fails, quickly try twisting his hand away as you would to remove someone's hand from your clothes (see page 83).

two-handed throat grip

This is much more dangerous than a one-handed throat grip because it is twice as strong. However, try not to let your fear overcome you as there is a simple, yet effective way of breaking free. Remember, if you practice this with your friends it will become an automatic response and could save your life.

1 PROTECT YOUR NECK As with the one-handed throat grip, immediately tense your neck muscles to shield your arteries. Pull your head back, away from your attacker. If you are able to, scream or shout as loud as you can.

try this...

GOUGING The thought of putting fingers and fingernails into an attacker's face or eyes can make people squeamish. However, it is important to remember that you are legally and morally allowed to do whatever is necessary to protect yourself, particularly if you are in a life-threatening situation.

The eyes are a sensitive area of the body, both physically and mentally. Gouging will almost certainly cause your attacker to let go with his hands. It may cause him temporary or even permanent blindness, but it will allow you to escape. When you gouge, either place your hands on each side of his face and put pressure on his eyes using your thumbs, or poke your fingers hard into both eyes. If you miss, drag your fingernails down his face.

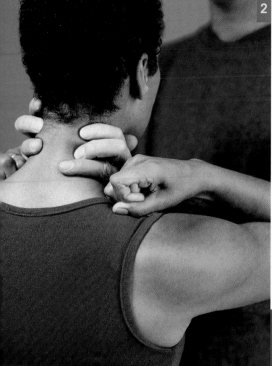

2 **GRAB YOUR ATTACKER'S LITTLE FINGERS** Try not to panic, but reach up to his hands as quickly as possible. Forcibly grab hold of his two little fingers and hold them very tightly, one in each of your hands. You'll find them at the base of your neck.

3 **RIP HIS HANDS AWAY** Using full strength, pull his little fingers outward, away from your neck. As many self-defense experts know, where the little fingers go, the hands will follow. Try it on yourself, and you'll see that it doesn't take much pressure on your little finger before it becomes painful. Imagine doing that with full force, and you'll understand why he will have to release you. If you keep hold of your attacker's hands, you will be able to escape by kneeing him in the groin.

3

throat grip from behind

This is a terrifying attack, made more frightening by the fact that you can't see your attacker. With eight fingers pressing on your neck, you also could suffer a broken windpipe, which is very serious, so there is a very real need to get your attacker's hands off you as quickly as possible. That this sort of thing happens and could happen to you should encourage you to practice this technique with a friend and learn to become more capable and confident of escaping.

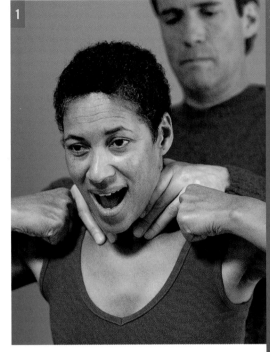

1 PROTECT YOUR NECK As with the other throat grips, tense your neck muscles by clenching your jaw and tucking your head into your neck. The muscles in your neck aren't very strong, but the resistance will give you a moment to breathe and prepare yourself. If you are standing, widen your feet a little and bend your knees for balance. If you can, scream to get attention.

2 GRAB YOUR ATTACKER'S LITTLE FINGERS Reach up with both hands and find his two little fingers, which will be at the base of your neck. Grab them tightly and rip them upward and back, behind your shoulders, without letting go. This will remove his hands from your throat.

ELBOW TO THE STOMACH Like your knees, your elbows are hard, bony surfaces that can deliver a powerful blow. They are one of the strongest parts of the body, and can be a useful weapon if you are struggling close to somebody, particularly if that person is behind you. To hit your attacker most effectively, clench the fist of the arm with which you are going to hit him. Place your other hand over the fist and use your free arm to push the elbow into his stomach. The blow should be a hard, fast jab so that your attacker has less chance to block it. Don't pull your arm too far forward before you strike or your attacker might see it coming. It doesn't matter where you aim. If you hit his ribs, you can cause great pain; If you hit him in the stomach, you could wind him, possibly even enough to stop him from following you.

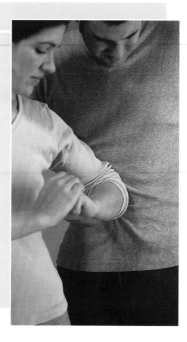

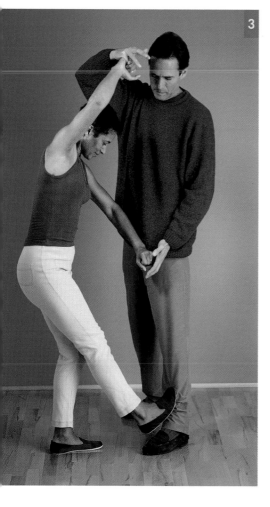

3

tactical tips

- Get an attacker's hands off your throat as quickly as possible.

- You may not be able to scream or shout when you are being choked or even afterward, so concentrate first on getting yourself free.

- Don't panic if you can't rip his hands away the first time; just keep trying until you do.

- Turn the element of surprise back on him by struggling wildly. Kick, elbow, and scream—your attacker will have been looking for an easy target, so it may be enough to frighten him.

3 FACE YOUR ATTACKER Keeping hold of your attacker's little fingers, twist around to face him, ducking under one of his arms—you may break his little fingers as you turn. If he's still holding on, kick him low and hard in the kneecaps, shins, or ankles. Keep kicking until he lets go.

neck choke from behind

This is a violent assault in which an attacker grabs you from behind, with one arm around your neck, pulling you in close and squeezing your throat. As with hand grips to the throat, it will hurt and can cause you to lose consciousness. This type of hold blocks your windpipe, not your arteries, so although you will find it difficult to breathe, you will have more time to act than if you were in a throat grip—perhaps as much as two minutes. You still need to move quickly, but don't panic or you won't be able to defend yourself effectively. Practice these techniques so they become instinctive.

2 TUCK YOUR HEAD IN By pulling down you will have moved his arm, even if only slightly. Tuck your chin into the space between his arm and your throat. Use your chin to lever his arm away a little more. This will stop him from choking you and allow you to breathe.

1 GRAB HIS ARM Using both hands, grab his sleeve or dig your fingers into his skin. Hold tightly, and with all your strength, pull his arm downward, away from your neck. At the same time, thrust your buttocks back into your attacker. This will prevent him from pulling you backward. You also could wind him.

3 **TURN AWAY FROM THE CHOKE** Using your whole body, twist around so that your face moves toward the hand holding your neck. Use your shoulder to lever his body away from you. Even if you can only twist partway, you will now be in a position to punch him hard in the groin or elbow him in the stomach.

tactical tips

- You have a lot more time to breathe than with a throat grip, so don't panic.

- If you can't grab the arm around your neck, pull hard on the sleeve—it will have the same effect—or if he is bare-skinned, dig your nails in and scratch—this will cause great pain, leave him marked, and you may get his skin and therefore his DNA underneath your nails for evidence.

- If you have your chin between his arm and your throat and his arm is bare, bite the arm as hard as you can. This should make him release you.

- Don't worry if his hold is so tight that you can't turn around. Stamp on his feet, kick back into his shins, or grab or punch back into his groin.

try this...

TESTICLE TWIST If a man is attacking you, one of his most sensitive areas will be his groin. It may be the last place that you want to touch him, but if you hurt him here, you can easily disable him. If his arm is around your neck, make sure that you don't take both your hands off his arm at the same time. One option is to punch him or hit his testicles with a knife hand (see page 89), but if you manage to grab hold, then you'll be more sure of hitting your target. To achieve this, simply feel backward until you have the correct spot, then grab and twist or squeeze. It won't take much pressure before he feels the pain and lets go.

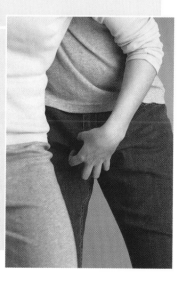

bear hugs and body wraps

These assaults are usually carried out by a man against a woman, since they require the attacker to be stronger than the victim. They may be used if someone wants to lift or drag you to a secluded place. Consequently, the fear is that such attacks are a prelude to a sexual assault. Your priorities are to attract attention as soon as possible and to stay in a public place.

front wraparound

An attacker looking for complete control may try to grab hold of your whole body. If your arms are trapped by your sides, it can make you feel particularly helpless. However, this is what your attacker wants. You need to believe in your abilities, as this is by no means a hopeless situation to be in.

1 PULL BACK Bend your knees to make it easier to balance and harder for your attacker to lift you. Lean away from him and jerk your body violently, showing him your resistance and strength. You may be able to shake him off or get an arm free to strike him.

tactical tips

- Don't panic if you find it hard to breathe with his arms around you. Take deep breaths and struggle hard against his grip—it will loosen. Never let him carry you away.

- Keep biting him until he lets go. He won't be able to do much while you're biting him.

try this...

FORWARD HEAD BUTT This is a good technique for a situation in which your face is very close to your attacker's. If his arms are around your waist or arms, he won't be able to stop you. Bring your head back slightly, look where you are aiming, and smash your forehead as hard as possible into his nose. Try to keep your nose down and to hit with your forehead; this is a hard surface and won't hurt you. The hit will, however, be agonizing for your attacker and will cause his eyes to water, giving you time to escape.

Women can be nervous about using head butts because they fear hurting themselves, or because they don't like the idea of possibly breaking another person's nose. However, as with many of these self-defense techniques, remember that you will only use such a move when desperate—and it can save your life.

2 BITE YOUR ATTACKER'S FACE With his arms around you, you will probably be on a level with his face. Overcome any distaste you may feel and bite his face wherever you can, as hard as you can (see page 106).

3 MAKE YOUR ESCAPE If you manage to force him back, bring your arm up into the space between you and strike him hard on the chin with the heel of your hand. This will knock him off balance and then give you the chance to break free.

one arm around the waist

By its nature, this type of attack will take you by surprise, and you need to act quickly before you are in your assailant's control. An attacker doing this might put his other hand around your mouth and nose to stop you from screaming and breathing. It is an unpleasant feeling, but don't let it overwhelm you. Keep your wits about you and remove that other hand so that you can breathe and scream for help as soon as possible.

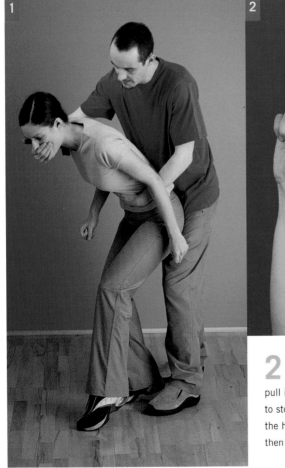

2 **RIP HIS HAND AWAY FROM YOUR MOUTH** Grab hold of his little finger as tightly as you can, and pull it up and outward away from your face. Keep hold to stop him from grabbing you again. Or you can bite the hand across your mouth as hard as you can and then scream loudly.

1 **RESIST HIS PULL** Thrust your buttocks back into your attacker's groin and stomach area. This will wind him and give you better balance. Lean forward away from him and use your body weight to resist the pull backward and stop him from lifting you.

3 **GET YOUR BODY FREE** Elbow hard and fast back into his stomach. As you swing, twist your body around slightly for more momentum. Alternatively, stamp down hard onto his ankle or punch back into his groin. Do anything you can to get away.

try this...

BACKWARD PUNCH If your attacker has hold of you from behind and you have an arm free, you can fight back. Although it is not easy to aim your strike, if you can manage to hit back into his face, your strike will cause him pain. It is also unlikely that your attacker will see this strike coming.

To punch backward, turn your head to get as good a view as possible of your target. Clench your hand into a fist, with your thumb outside the fingers. Keeping your elbow bent and low, snap your fist straight back into your attacker's nose, eye, or jaw. Try to hit using the knuckles of your forefinger and middle finger, rather than the flat of your hand, which may hurt you. Unlike the punch to face (see page 91), bend your wrist slightly backward as you hit.

bear hug with arms pinned

In this type of hold, an attacker can squeeze very tightly, and it will wind you. An assailant who grabs you in this way may well try to pick you up off the ground and take you to a secluded spot. Keep a clear head and try to keep breathing. You will be able to loosen his grip.

1 **SCREAM AND STRUGGLE** As soon as you are grabbed, start struggling violently by jerking forward and back using all your body weight. Try to break your arms free by pulling your hands up and out from his grasp or by biting and scratching his arms if you can reach.

try this...

SCRATCHING AND BITING Don't be afraid to draw blood from an assailant. Use your nails and teeth if you have a chance to; it may be enough to break free. In addition, if you scratch deep enough, you might get lumps of his skin trapped under your nails. Although you may want to get rid of this as soon as possible, don't wash away chunks of skin or blood, as the police will be able to use this to get a profile of an attacker's DNA as evidence. If your face is close to any exposed skin on your attacker, don't be afraid to bite. It may be repellent, but don't worry about catching anything—the risk of this is very slim compared to the risk of serious injury, rape, or even death if you don't bite him.

2 KICK WITH BOTH FEET If he has lifted you off the ground, use both your feet and start kicking backward into his legs. Even if you feel yourself connect, keep kicking as hard as you can. If you are wearing high heels, so much the better. Jab the heels into his shins and kneecaps.

3 PERFORM A BACKWARD HEAD BUTT This move should be fast. Bend your head forward slightly and then snap it back sharply into his face. You should catch his nose, chin, or cheek. Don't worry about hurting your head; it will be much more painful for your attacker than for you.

bear hug with arms free

Although your priority in most situations is to stay on your feet so that you can make your escape, an attacker grabbing you from behind like this will often want to drag you somewhere quiet and more secluded. This is why you need to make yourself as immovable as possible by turning yourself into a dead weight and dropping heavily downward. Alternatively, you can achieve immobility by grabbing hold of a stable object, such as a fence, fire hydrant, tree, or lamppost.

2 DROP TO THE FLOOR If your attacker is still pulling you, relax your legs completely. Although this might sound like the last thing you want to do, it means that your attacker now has to lift all of your body weight to move you.

1 REACT IMMEDIATELY Struggle as soon as you are grabbed. Your attacker is likely to want to pull you backward, but try to resist by pulling forward. Grab hold of something if you can.

try this...

ELBOW TO THE FACE An elbow strike to the head area can daze an attacker and may even knock him unconscious. It is particularly useful if your attacker manages to pick you up off the ground so that your arms and shoulders are level with his face. As with any elbow strike, the trick is to move quickly. This will give the strike more momentum. Twist your body as you swing to build up speed, and aim for the jawbone, face, or temples. For extra strength and stability, you can link your hands before you swing.

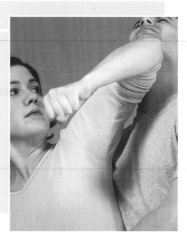

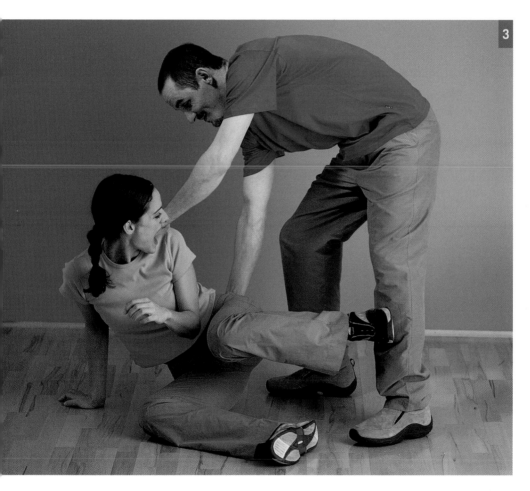

3 KEEP YOUR ATTACKER AWAY If you are on the floor, don't let him near you, but support yourself on one hand and kick him. Aim for his shins and kneecaps, not his groin, as he may grab your leg. Shout loudly to attract attention.

defense on the ground

If you are ever attacked, you should try to avoid falling to the floor as it will take you longer to escape. Also, it is harder to fight somebody from a prone position. However, it's not impossible. If you should find yourself on the ground, use some of the following techniques and try to get up as quickly as possible.

falling on your front

If you are running to escape an attacker, it's not uncommon to trip and fall. Unfortunately, this can give your attacker the moment he needs to catch up to you. If you quickly pull yourself into a ball, this can protect you from harm and allow you to prepare your escape.

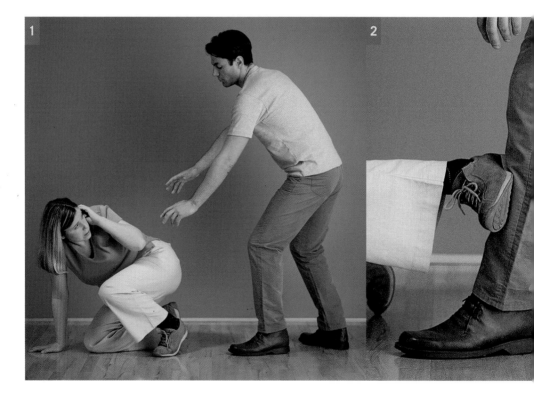

1 PROTECT YOURSELF Either curl over on both knees or get into a crouching position on your feet. This will protect your more vulnerable body parts from kicks. It also puts you into a good sprinting position. Keep an eye on your attacker until you see a chance to escape from him.

2 KICK YOUR ATTACKER If he does grab hold of you, kick back hard into his shins and kneecaps. Don't kick too high, or he could grab your leg.

attacker on top of you

In some situations where you are on the ground, your attacker will remain standing so that he can drag or kick you easily. If an attacker gets on top of you while you are in this position, it is likely to be a sexual attack. There is no right or wrong answer as to what you should do in this situation. You may feel that you risk greater injury or even death if you struggle and that your attacker won't injure you if you do as he asks. On the other hand, you may think he is lying and will hurt you anyway. In this case, a struggle could be your best option.

If an attacker is heavy or strong, it can be difficult to lift or roll him off you. In this case, you have a choice: You can struggle immediately to prevent him from getting any closer, or you can wait and strike when he is vulnerable—often when he is fumbling with his zipper or when he is fully exposed.

1 USE YOUR VOICE AND HANDS Scream and shout in your attacker's ear. Get your hands free to pull his hair, scratch his face, or gouge his eyes.

2 BITE HIS FACE OR EARS If your arms are being held, lean forward and aim for his cheeks, nose, or ears. If you can't reach, bite his neck.

3 CHOOSE YOUR MOMENT If your attacker sits up to undo his pants, punch him as hard as you can in the groin or face. If you can, grab a piece of wood or a brick, and hit him with it. This should knock him off balance.

attacker astride you

If you fall to the ground and your attacker is standing astride you, it may be because he wants to drag you away somewhere or get on top of you. From this position, your attacker may also be able to kick your sides and stomach, which can cause internal damage. You should try to kick out quickly to prevent your attacker from getting any closer until you have a chance to get up and escape.

2 KICK TO THE SIDE Lean on the elbow closest to the floor. Place your other hand on the floor in front of you for balance. Lift your top leg about 6 in. (15 cm) and bring the knee up toward your chest. Now kick with full force into your attacker's legs. Keep facing your attacker and kicking out to prevent him from getting near you. If you need to move around, use your elbow to pivot your body.

1 KICK YOUR ATTACKER'S LEGS Keep your kicks low, aiming at his shins, kneecaps, and ankles. Try not to aim at his groin, or he may grab your foot. Look at where you are aiming, because he will move around to avoid your kicks. If you kick out hard enough, you should force him to move to the side. Scream loudly.

3 **DEFEND YOUR OTHER SIDE** If your attacker moves behind you, roll over onto your other side and continue to kick. From this position, you should be able to keep your attacker away from you while you use your elbow and hands to help push yourself up onto your feet. Practice this move at home and switch sides so that you are just as efficient at kicking with both legs.

4

personal attacks

If you were mugged, stalked, sexually assaulted, or abused by your partner, how would you cope? Lessen your fears by finding out what such crimes and behavior patterns can involve and, if you have been affected, learn the best ways to stay safe, find help, and get on with your life.

muggings

Being robbed in the street not only results in a loss of property, but also may be accompanied by violence and can leave you with mixed and painful emotions. If you follow the precautions in Chapter 2 you will reduce your chances of being mugged. But a look at what happens before and after an attack can lessen your fear of becoming a victim and may even help you make sense of things if you are ever mugged.

what street robberies involve

Typically, muggers are teens or young adults who attack people for their possessions or money. They want these things, so they steal in order to get them. Some muggers are drug users who steal to feed a habit—the money is just a means to an end. Many muggers work in gangs, and for them, the element of daring each other and showing off provides an added motivation.

In many cases, muggers don't set out to hurt their victims; the focus of the crime is not the person they attack but her possessions. On the other hand, muggers rarely have compassion for those they attack and may even see them as weak and inferior. They may even justify an attack by saying that the victim shouldn't have reacted the way she did.

what makes a victim?

When questioned, experienced muggers often describe similar reasons for choosing their victims. Because muggers don't want to get hurt, people who don't seem likely to fight back or give chase, such as the elderly or children, are often popular targets. Also, muggers are opportunists; they will attack people who seem to have something of value, such as jewelry, a briefcase, a laptop, or a cell phone. This is why you should always look confident, be aware of your surroundings, and conceal items of value.

how should I react?

In many cases, you won't have time to make a decision and will just react instinctively. However, if you do have time to think, you should follow the guidelines on page 72. If you are in any doubt, hand over your property calmly in an attempt to avoid violence and get away as quickly as possible. Remember, your health and well-being are much more precious than any possession.

WHAT HAPPENS WHEN...

MUGGERS ATTACK

Most street robbers want as little resistance as possible, and this influences how they approach their victims. Many will try to use the element of surprise—perhaps running up to a victim from behind and snatching what they want as they continue to run. Others will try to intimidate their victims with loud, abusive language, sometimes accompanied by physical assaults or the threat of a weapon. This will rarely be a personal attack on the victim—muggers often don't even remember what their victims look like.

If muggers work in groups, attacks can be slightly different. One may try to distract the victim, while another grabs what's wanted. Or they may surround the victim and either threaten her until they get what they want or two or more will hold the victim's hands while another searches for items of value.

Muggers try to surprise people. If you're suspicious of somebody, turn to face him to deter an attack.

the aftermath of an attack

After a mugging, some people are afraid to report it or think there's no point because the criminals will get away with it in the end. However, you should always report a crime, even if you weren't injured. Muggers tend to stick to the same areas, and some may be known to the police already. Your report may be the final piece of evidence they require to secure a conviction. If your keys were stolen, talk to the police before you go home, as the muggers may be able to find out where you live.

the emotional response

Any mugging or attempted mugging, whether you're physically injured or not, will have an effect on you. You may feel a number of things, all of which are normal reactions, such as:

- **ANGER** That it happened to you and that the attacker might get away with it can make you mad. You might feel a need for revenge.
- **ANXIETY** You may lose confidence in your ability to look after yourself and fear that something similar might happen again.
- **DISTRUST** You may be more suspicious of other people, whether they're strangers, the police, or your family and friends.
- **ISOLATION** You may not know anyone who has been through such an attack, and this can leave you feeling very alone.
- **SHAME** You may be upset because you were singled out, couldn't fight off your attacker, or didn't use any defensive techniques.

It's important to remember that everyone recovers at different rates. Your initial feelings can last for several days, weeks, or months, or they may fade and be replaced by other feelings.

It's not uncommon to suffer symptoms of depression, such as sleeplessness, irritability, and withdrawal, for a long time after the event. You may wish to talk through the attack repeatedly or not talk about it at all. However, there are things you can do to help yourself. Reporting the attack will be the first stage in getting over your ordeal. After that, eating a healthy diet, drinking alcohol only in moderation, and getting plenty of exercise and rest will help.

seeking professional help

While you may be a confident and controlled person in everyday life, you should accept that muggings aren't ordinary. If you're not coping and your feelings are affecting your work, home life, or relationships, victim support groups in your area should be able to help. Not only can they provide assurance and refer you to counseling, they also should be able to advise you on the court system. Speak to the police or your doctor for contact information.

stalking and harassment

The U.S. Department of Justice has estimated that 8 percent of women and 2 percent of men have been stalked at some point in their lives—that's about 1.4 million victims each year. In Canada, according to Statistics Canada, there were 5382 incidents of stalking in 1999—that's up 32 percent from the previous three years.

what constitutes stalking?

Legal definitions of stalking—also called "criminal harassment"—vary depending on where you live, but, generally, the laws prohibit somebody from deliberately acting in a way that causes another person to fear for her safety. In some areas, stalkers can be punished even if they don't intend to scare or hurt the victim.

Stalking is commonly triggered by unrequited romantic attention, sometimes at the end of a

failed relationship. However, there are rarer cases in which the stalker is suffering from a mental illness. A famous case of a delusional stalker is John Hinckley Jr., who shot President Ronald Reagan in an attempt to gain the attention of actress Jodie Foster.

Often, a stalker may start out making a few phone calls or sending a few e-mails to a person or may "coincidentally" run into her on the street. Stalkers who then feel rejected may start to intimidate their victims with threatening letters, telephone messages, or "presents," such as dead flowers. A stalker may start to watch his victim's house, sometimes taking photographs. In extreme cases, stalkers may become so angry that they vandalize property, threaten pets, or commit physical violence or even murder.

It's important to remember, though, that not all cases follow the same pattern; often stalkers go no further than the first stage and their interest simply dies out. However, if you become a victim of stalking, you should always treat it seriously and act to protect yourself.

how stalking affects victims

Even if the threat of violence seems low, stalking is frightening and, because of its relentlessness, often emotionally draining for victims. Psychological damage has included symptoms like paranoia, agoraphobia, and eating disorders. In addition, stalking victims' lifestyles can be adversely affected, causing some, for example, to lose time from work.

Record all incidents from the beginning. Make a note of the date, time, location, witnesses, and full details of any suspicious behavior, contact, threats, or crimes.

action plan

If you find you have a stalker, make it clear you don't want his attention in plain and simple terms and in front of others. After that, avoid communicating with him in any way. Tell friends, family, and colleagues what is happening—they'll be able to stay with you if you feel threatened. Point out the stalker or give them a description and a photo—but only if you can get one without the stalker's knowledge.

keep a record

If you feel you may have to go to the police, you'll need to show them evidence before they'll take action. Take a note of all incidents, but be careful not to write anything that you wouldn't wish the stalker to hear, as it may be read out in court if your case goes that far. Keep any letters or presents from the stalker in zippered plastic bags, and try not to handle them too much. Copy or photograph them before turning them over to the police. Also, print out e-mails and keep tapes of answering machine messages. Take photos of destroyed property or injuries.

seek help

About half of all stalking cases aren't reported to the police, probably because the victims don't take it seriously or because they fear that nobody will believe them. However, more and more law enforcement agencies are recognizing the seriousness of this crime. Even if the police can't help you immediately, they should be able to give advice about security and providing evidence, as well as information about any stalking or domestic violence groups in your area. If you are ever in immediate danger, go to a police station, the house of friends or family, or a domestic violence shelter. If you are trapped in the house, call the police.

STEP UP SECURITY

If you are being stalked, check that you are following all the security basics covered in Chapter 2 and take a few extra precautions.

☐ **Avoid being watched** Close all curtains and blinds when you're at home.

☐ **Block your address** Contact your local vehicle and voter registration organizations to check that your contact information is not available to the public. Use a post office box or a friend's address for correspondence. If you're a victim of cyberstalking, get a new log-on name and password from your Internet service provider or get a new account.

☐ **Change your routine** On regular journeys, vary your route. The group Survivors of Stalking (see page 170) recommends that if you think your car is being followed, you should take four left or four right turns to check. If you are being followed, don't drive home, but keep your doors locked and drive to a police station and sound your horn to attract help.

☐ **Check your car** If you think your car may have been tampered with, check the wheels, under the hood, and under the car for anything that looks suspicious, such as loose nuts or wires, leaking fluid, or unusual parts. Don't drive it if you think something is wrong.

☐ **Check your garbage** Shred all personal or official correspondence—a stalker may go through your bins.

☐ **Consider moving** This is an extreme step, but according to the National Violence Against Women Survey, this is one of the most effective ways to stop a stalker if all else fails.

☐ **Make an emergency plan** If you're worried about being attacked at home, think of places you could go for help, such as a friend's house or a local domestic violence shelter. Pack a suitcase including items that you might have in an evacuation kit (see page 21). Always keep a full tank of gas in the car.

sexual offenses

The U.S.-based Rape, Abuse, and Incest National Network (RAINN) calculates that someone in the United States is sexually assaulted every two minutes. Statistics Canada has estimated that almost half of Canadian women have been sexually assaulted in their lifetimes. Exact figures are hard to determine because the large majority of attacks go unreported, often due to the complex emotional upset that such crimes cause. Avoiding attack is covered elsewhere in this book. This section looks at coping with the crime itself and the aftermath.

what constitutes a crime?

The terms "rape" and "sexual assault" have different definitions depending on which country, state, or province you are in. However, it is generally a crime to force anyone to take part in sexual acts, which can include vaginal or anal penetration; oral sex; and touching or fondling of breasts or genitals. The force involved might include actual physical harm or the threat of injury to the victim or another person. It's also a crime to commit these acts on somebody who is unable to give consent, for example, if that person is asleep or under the influence of drugs or alcohol.

STREETSMART

DON'T LET YOURSELF BE TAKEN AWAY Do everything in your power to prevent an attacker from dragging you to a secondary place—a car, building, or side street. This takes you away from other people and gives him control over you and the environment. He may have prepared the place with items to restrain or hurt you.

Another category of rape or sexual assault involves sex with a minor, which is a crime even if the child or teen consents. The exact age of a minor varies depending on where you live. For information on child abuse, see page 134.

The law also varies on who may be the victims of rape or sexual assault. In some areas, both males and females can be victims of both, but in others, rape may only be committed against females, and attacks against males would be termed sexual assault.

what is acquaintance rape?

Random attacks by strangers are much rarer than the media might suggest, and many sources agree that sexual assaults by people known to their victims are much more common—1997 figures from the U.S. Bureau of Justice Statistics report that acquaintance rape accounted for 77 percent of sexual assault cases. The Canadian-based organization Education Wife Assault (see page 171) reports that victims know their attackers in 69 percent of cases. The offenders might be anyone from friends or neighbors to health-care providers or teachers. These attacks also can occur when a man or woman is on a date, and the attacks aren't confined to first dates—many take place on a fourth or fifth date. In fact, rape or sexual assault can be committed in any situation in which one of the couple doesn't want sexual contact, even if the two involved have kissed or had sex before. A husband can be convicted of sexually assaulting his wife, even if he is still living with her and separation or divorce proceedings have not begun. Such an attack is often tied to domestic violence (see page 124).

Protect yourself against such assaults by being wary of new encounters or unusual behavior in a friend, relative, or colleague. Don't invite anyone back to your home or give out your address until you know him well. If anybody makes unwanted advances, leave him in no doubt that you're not interested and that "no" means just that. When out and about, don't drink more than you know you can handle, and don't accept drinks from a stranger or leave your drink unattended—"date rape" drugs are tasteless and colorless (see page 37).

what motivates an attacker?

Interviews with rapists have revealed their main motivation is to exert control over others; this crime has nothing to do with desire, passion, or love. Many rapists have severe psychological problems and may have experienced sexual abuse as a child. They may show their desire for sexual dominance by a hatred of women or by condoning violence in relationships. However, these signs are not easy to identify, and rapists may appear to be "normal," functioning members of a community. Also, latent problems can become exaggerated with drugs or alcohol.

Avoid vulnerable situations when on a date. Stay in public places and don't go back to your date's home. If you feel unsafe at any point, make an excuse to leave.

action plan

Despite our best efforts to stay safe, attacks do happen. If you are worried about how best to handle an attack, review the following information. If you have experienced rape or sexual assault, knowing what others have been through can help your recovery process.

reacting to an attack

Many people wonder what they would and should do during a sexual assault. As with other personal attacks, your reaction is difficult to predict and depends on your physical and emotional state, the situation, and how the attacker behaves toward you. Only you can assess those factors and decide on the most appropriate action.

Always try to bear in mind the basic principles of defense (see page 72). Reacting immediately by screaming, shouting, struggling, and using defensive moves gives you a good chance of attracting help and may be enough to convince an attacker that you are too difficult to control. However, shock or fear—particularly if your attacker has a weapon—may immobilize you temporarily. But this doesn't mean that you don't have other options. You could wait for the right moment to shout out or fight back, such as when your attacker has put his weapon down or is undoing his clothes.

If your attacker tells you that he won't hurt you if you don't scream or resist, you might decide that doing what he says is the best way to survive, particularly if he has a weapon. Consider, however, that this involves trusting your attacker to keep his word, and that he will walk away after the attack. He could hurt you

further in order to scare you and discourage you from going to the police. Admittedly, there is a risk also when you fight back that it may anger your attacker and cause him to retaliate, but this should be weighed against the risk of not doing anything and being hurt anyway.

Many people who are raped, however, choose not to struggle or are unable to because they are paralyzed with fear. Even if they fight back, it is still common for victims to doubt themselves after an attack and question whether there was more they could have done. You should never feel guilty for encouraging an attack or "letting it happen." The rapist is the one to blame; you didn't ask to be attacked.

help a victim

If your friend, partner, or a member of your family has been sexually assaulted, your support will be important. Here are some ways to offer it, according to the U.K.-based Rape Crisis Federation (www.rapecrisis.co.uk).

- Give her time. Don't rush her to talk to you, and be patient with her recovery, which may take years.

- Be compassionate and unconditional in your support of her. Believe what she tells you. Don't push your opinions, but help by discussing issues.

- Help her understand that it was not her fault and that the blame belongs with the attacker.

- Be on hand to help out with such things as housework, but only if she wants you to do it.

- Reassure a partner that she is still attractive. Don't pressure her into further sexual contact, but allow her to control the pace.

Be available to offer comfort whenever the victim needs it. She may feel that she is taking up your time or is a burden to you; reassure her that she isn't.

reporting an attack to the police

There are a few reasons why some people choose not to report sexual attacks. They include shame and embarrassment, fear of retaliation, or the victim's belief that she was somehow to blame. However, reporting the crime can be beneficial; it can fulfill a sense of justice, help people feel safer, and help prevent the rapist from attacking anyone else.

Your first priority after an attack should be to get to a safe place from where you can call the police, an ambulance, or a friend or family member. Although your instincts may be to wash yourself as soon as possible, you should avoid this, as well as changing your clothes or even brushing your teeth, until you have been examined and told that you can do so. But if you have washed, don't let that stop you from going to the police; there still may be evidence they can use—semen can stay in the vagina for up to seven days. The police will arrange for a medical examination, which can be conducted by a female doctor at your request.

Even if you don't go to the police, you should visit your doctor or the hospital so that any injuries can be treated, and you can discuss the need for emergency contraception and the risks of sexually transmitted diseases.

the emotional aftermath

Whatever the circumstances of a rape or sexual assault, the impact can be massive. People's responses are highly individual, and the feelings you encounter may change as time passes.

Initially, you may be scared, disbelieving, or numb. Some people feel distanced and matter-of-fact; others cry hysterically and can't stop. Self-blame is a very common reaction and can be a barrier to accepting that what happened was actually a crime. After time, some people

WHAT HAPPENS WHEN...

YOU SUFFER FROM POST-TRAUMATIC STRESS DISORDER

This psychological disorder, which arises as a result of exposure to a terrifying experience, such as rape or sexual assault, can be disabling and may not appear until some months or years after the event. It may be triggered by any small detail that reminds the person of the event, such as sounds, smells or the anniversary of the attack. Symptoms include flashbacks, disturbing dreams, depression, irritability, anger, guilt, or deliberately blocking out the event. If you fear that you may be suffering, speak to a doctor or counselor. Treatment may include behavioral therapy, group therapy, or controlled reliving of the event. Medication may be prescribed.

attempt to cope by becoming insular and uncommunicative, while others become promiscuous. Rape or sexual assault can lead also to post-traumatic stress disorder (see box, above).

Even if you believe at first that you can cope with this alone, the most effective way of dealing with such an attack is to acknowledge what happened and seek help from a counselor or psychologist as soon as possible after an attack. The recovery process may take weeks, months, or even years. Counseling will help you work through your feelings, and you may be prescribed medication to help with sleep problems or getting on with your daily life. Find information on counseling through your doctor, the police, or help groups (see page 170).

Sexual assault can affect partners and family members in equally powerful ways. They may feel angry and want revenge or feel inadequate for not being able to protect a loved one. No matter how unwillingly, some partners may even blame the victim for not stopping the attack. Counseling can provide an outlet for these feelings. For tips on how to help a victim, see opposite.

domestic violence

Many people never dream that domestic violence might happen to them or to somebody they know, yet it is extremely common. In the United States, statistics from the Justice Department suggest that up to 4 million women suffer because of it each year. In Canada, the 1999 General Social Survey estimated that 1.2 million men and women had faced some form of violence in their relationships in the previous five years. These figures, however, can only hint at the full story of domestic violence, simply because it manifests itself in so many different ways and so often goes unreported.

WHAT HAPPENS WHEN...

CHILDREN ARE INVOLVED

Links have been established between domestic violence and child abuse. The U.S. National Domestic Violence Hotline reports that child abuse occurs in 30 to 60 percent of families in which there is domestic violence. Some abusers will use a child as a weapon against the other partner, threatening to hurt the child if the victim complains. Sometimes, a child may be deliberately injured or abused during an attack.

Even when a child is not at immediate risk of abuse, domestic violence can be extremely traumatic. Individuals respond differently: Some children may become depressed and withdrawn, while others may engage in anti-social behavior. There is a high risk, too, that children may repeat the violence when they grow up. Even if the parents attempt to hide spousal abuse, children are very perceptive and usually know what is happening.

forms of abuse

Abusive behavior toward partners or spouses can occur at any stage of a relationship: when dating, married, or when going through a separation. All cases will take one or more of the following forms:

- **MENTAL ABUSE** This can include possessive behavior, emotional blackmail, or verbal abuse. One partner may take excessive control over how the other spends her time or money, or may seek to prevent the partner from working. He may embarrass her in front of others or belittle her accomplishments. Abusers often try to isolate the victim from friends and family.
- **PHYSICAL VIOLENCE** Aggressive behavior can range from restraining, pushing, or physically intimidating the victim to severe beating and life-threatening violence.
- **SEXUAL ABUSE** This is when either partner is forced into unwanted sexual activity, even if married to or in a long-standing relationship with the other.

who commits domestic violence?

Not all abusers are overtly aggressive, and they often can appear pleasant or charming to outsiders and even to their victims. Nor are their victims weak; domestic violence can happen to anyone and cuts across all economic, regional, racial, and professional lines. It is often assumed that only men are perpetrators of domestic violence and women are the only victims. But men also can be victims—at the hands of female partners or in same-sex relationships.

Those who abuse others sometimes blame their actions on outside circumstances, such as stress, alcohol, or their victim's behavior. However, abusers are responsible for the harm they cause. Their problems are usually more deep-seated than they might realize, arising, for example, out of the perpetrator's low self-esteem or feeling of powerlessness. In many cases, those who commit violence often experienced it in their childhoods, either as a victim or witness. When they later commit physical or mental abuse, it can give them a sense of control and self-esteem, particularly if they suffer from extreme emotional highs and lows.

action plan

Victims of domestic violence often take a long time to break free of a destructive relationship. However, abuse is rarely a one-time event; it's essential to break the chain as soon as possible.

facing the barriers

Individuals who stay in abusive relationships should never be criticized or made to feel weak, as there are many real and complex reasons why it may be difficult to leave.

People suffering from domestic abuse may take a while to acknowledge their victim status in the first place. Victims frequently hold themselves to be in some way responsible, and, even if they don't blame themselves, they may try to rationalize their abuser's behavior by blaming outside factors, such as stress. Also, during non-aggressive phases, abusers may be loving, romantic, or vulnerable. This can lead a victim to overlook violent or upsetting episodes. But an abusive relationship rarely heals by itself. It's important to recognize that you are a victim, that you are not responsible, and that no one deserves to be assaulted, abused, or humiliated.

The thought of leaving such a relationship can be as frightening as the thought of staying.

If you are suffering in an abusive relationship, it's important to recognize that you need to take action. For some ideas on emergency plans, see page 127.

Sometimes, there may seem to be no real alternative—if, for example, the victim doesn't have a job and is financially dependent. The options can seem particularly restricted when the person has been isolated from friends and family. Also, victims may fear that an attempt to leave could cause their abusers to become more violent or manipulative. However, it is usually the case that the longer the victim stays in an abusive relationship, the more frequent and severe the abuse becomes.

Many victims fear losing custody of their children if they leave a relationship, and abusers often capitalize on this, using it as a threat to control their victims. However, it is not the policy of social service agencies to remove children for this reason. Other victims feel that single-parent families are unacceptable, and that a violent or controlling parent is better than none. In reality, however, this is rarely the case. Children living in households where there is domestic violence are at risk themselves of trauma, depression, or injury (see page 124).

seeking help

If you are suffering from domestic violence, bear in mind that you are not alone, and there are avenues open to you. Telling someone what is happening is the first big psychological step. The police are now very aware of domestic violence and treat it seriously. If you are faced with an emergency, the police should be your first contact. Most forces have specially trained officers and can assist you with medical aid and transport you to a safe place. If you just need someone to talk to, or to find out what your options are next, the police will be able to put you in touch with someone who can help.

If you don't want to go to the police and feel unable to confide in family or friends, consider contacting a victims' support group. Many groups exist, both to offer advice and, if necessary, give shelter. Local law enforcement agencies, libraries, and your doctor will have information on shelters in your area.

Many sites on the Internet also offer opportunities for victims to find support, share stories, and discover more specific information. Some sites to try in the United States are: www.ndvh.org, endabuse.org, and www.ncadv.org. In Canada, try www.hc-sc.gc.ca and www.womanabuseprevention.com. Also see page 170. Bear in mind that Web sites you visit will be stored in your computer. If you're worried that your abuser may be checking on your computer activity, and you want to play it safe, don't use your home computer to find these sites. Instead, use a friend's computer or one at your local library or at work.

make an emergency plan

The U.S.-based National Center for Victims of Crime (see page 170) has compiled suggestions for what you can do to improve your safety. Here are a few tips on avoiding violence.

- **IDENTIFY DANGER SIGNS** Work out the symptoms of your partner's aggression so you're prepared to defend yourself or leave the home as soon as they appear.
- **FIND SAFE ROOMS** Think of areas in the home which are weapon-free and where there is access to the outside and try to get there if an argument occurs. The kitchen, bathroom, and garage should be avoided.
- **MINIMIZE INJURIES** If violence is unavoidable, get into a corner and curl up in a ball, protecting your face with your hands. Steer clear of the children.

help a victim

If you suspect that a friend or colleague is at risk, here are a few ways that you can help.

- A victim of abuse should be encouraged to express her fears, hurt, and anger. Avoid being judgmental—the situation may be highly complex.
- Comfort her. Even if your friend or colleague doesn't want to contact anyone, it is empowering to know that there are others in the same situation and that support is available.
- Keep yourself safe. Never try to intervene in a fight, but call the police. Only offer refuge if the abusive partner doesn't know your address. If he does, help the victim find other emergency shelter.
- Be patient. Don't push the victim into leaving a relationship or going to the police. Some victims suffer for years, and during this time other friends and family may drift away, so try to stick with it.

- **BRIEF YOUR CHILDREN** Tell your children to hide in a lockable room such as the bathroom or go to a trusted neighbor if they hear shouting. Teach them how to call 911.

- **PREPARE EMERGENCY CONTACTS** Ask a trusted neighbor to call the police if she hears suspicious noises, and ask your friends if they would shelter you if you need to escape. Develop a code word that you can use on the phone to signal that you need help.

- **PLAN YOUR ESCAPE** Pack a suitcase, and consider including items that you might have in an evacuation kit (see page 21). Keep this at the house of a trusted friend and ask her to hold any money that you can put aside. Keep a full tank of gas in the car.

- **KEEP A RECORD** Make a journal of all incidents, including dates, but keep it where your partner can't find it. If you visit a doctor or an emergency room, make sure your visit is documented.

Even after you leave an abusive relationship, you will need to protect yourself. Consider all the places where your ex-partner may be able to find you. For example, change the route you take to work or when dropping the kids off at school and consider shopping in a different area. Be careful to whom you give your new address. If you get a restraining order, give copies to your employer, neighbors, and the school, along with a photograph of your ex-partner. If the order is broken, call the police.

Offer practical support. If there is no chance that the abuser can find out, allow a victim to use your computer, phone, or address to research help groups.

5

child and teenage **safety**

The safety habits you teach your children will last a lifetime. Provide young children with techniques for dealing with strangers. With school-age kids, learn how best to broach the subjects of gangs, drugs, and alcohol. And when your teens go off to college, be ready to give advice on campus security and keeping their belongings safe.

safety begins at home

Striking a good balance between safeguarding your children and being overprotective can sometimes be difficult. You don't want to scare your children, but you need to give them sufficient information, guidance, and support to keep them out of trouble when you're not around. Knowing that you've eliminated the potential danger spots in your home also should enable you to feel confident that your children will be safe at all times.

teach your children

Discuss safety issues when your children are old enough to understand the dangers they may face. If you give a child a bicycle or cell phone, for example, discuss why it's best to give it up if someone tries to steal it. And tell your children from an early age that it is never appropriate for an adult to touch private parts of their bodies and that if this happens they should speak to you or another adult they trust (see page 134). Teachers are an excellent source of information, and it can be worth finding out what the school has already taught your children about safety.

The important thing is to be honest; avoiding a subject doesn't protect your children from the consequences—they might get information from other sources, and it might confuse or scare them if it doesn't come from you. Try using a news story to open a discussion. Although you may not like introducing such horrific topics as kidnapping, pedophilia, and murder to your kids, it is possible to talk about them in an instructive and reassuring way.

Discuss safety when kids are relaxed and calm, such as when eating dinner or playing; they're less likely to be scared by what you tell them.

Emphasize that bad things rarely happen, and tell them that kids can defend themselves and escape from strangers (see page 137). If your children initiate a discussion, listen and show that you take their concerns seriously.

Teach emergency procedures, such as how to call for help (see page 166) if there is an accident or fire. Also help your children learn how to contact you.

managing conflict

Like adults, children face many conflicts in their lives, from simple things, such as fights over property, to more involved arguments over privacy and staying out late. Conflict can make children angry and frustrated, which sometimes causes them to act irresponsibly or get into fights or other trouble. You need to discuss with your children nonviolent ways of working through their problems if you want to ensure they become and remain "model citizens."

Begin by telling your children that not all conflict is bad; what's important is how you deal with it. Tell them that hurting people is never a solution to a problem, and that the only way they are going to work it out and feel better is to think, talk, and listen. Here are some important steps in reaching a resolution.

- **CALM DOWN** Explain to your children that when we get angry or excited, we often experience a surge of adrenaline (see page 15), which can make us feel more aggressive or impulsive. Suggest ways that they can calm down and think, such as taking a few deep breaths and counting to 10.
- **EXPRESS FEELINGS** Teach your children how to identify their emotions; how do they feel when they're irritated, annoyed, angry, upset, or hurt? Help them talk about these feelings and explain that others feel like that, too.

Self-defense or martial arts classes are great places for kids to practice techniques and build confidence. You also should teach them the techniques in Chapter 3.

- **LISTEN AND EMPATHIZE** Point out that it's easy during an argument to be thinking only of what you want to say next. Help your children recognize other people's feelings and points of view so that your children learn how to treat others with respect.
- **DISCUSS A SOLUTION** Tell your kids that they shouldn't run away from a problem but do their best to solve it. Teach them how to find alternatives and compromises.

set a good example

Children learn how to deal with anger and conflict from what they see their parents, peers, and teachers do, and from what they see in the media. You need to set a good example when resolving family problems. If you have to discipline your child, explain the reasons and don't yell or use physical punishment; consider banning TV or computer games for a while or restricting your child's allowance. Consider also the messages they get from TV (see page 138).

STREETSMART

TEACH CULTURAL DIVERSITY Explain that people of different races, countries, and backgrounds may have habits and ideas that are "different" but equally valid to yours—for example, in their religion, clothes, or food. If they understand this, they may be less likely to tease or bully others.

131

organizing child care

Most parents need to arrange care for their children at some time, whether full time while away at work or for the occasional night out. Here are some safety issues to keep in mind.

employing baby-sitters

In the United States and Canada there is no legal minimum age for baby-sitters, but many child welfare agencies recommend that baby-sitters are at least 12 or 13 years old. Because teens mature at different rates, it is a good idea to interview potential sitters before you leave them alone with your children. Check that they seem happy and relaxed with your kids. Ask about their child care experience, whether they have taken baby-sitting courses, and how they would handle specific emergencies.

give baby-sitter guidelines

Provide your sitter with safety instructions before you go out. Make sure you include the following:

- Give your full name and contact details so the sitter knows where she can reach you.

- List your full address and phone number so that the sitter has them on hand if she needs to make an emergency call.

- Provide your children's full names, birth dates, health insurance details, and health information, such as allergies and medical conditions.

- Have a list of important numbers posted by the phone (see page 17).

- Make it clear whether she can bring a friend. Tell her what to say if the phone rings. And emphasize that no alcohol is allowed.

employing nannies and au pairs

For full-time care, you'll need to hire a qualified nanny—au pairs may have no training or experience in child care. Use a reputable placement agency to find a nanny, or hire someone whom a friend has used in the past. The U.S.-based International Nanny Association recommends that you interview prospective candidates at least twice. You should check references yourself, and, if possible, visit families for whom the nanny has worked.

using full- or part-time day care

Check with your local authorities for registered child care centers in your area, and visit as many as you can to see what is offered. Consider the following:

- **APPEARANCE OF KIDS** Do the children look happy, busy, and well cared for?
- **CLEANLINESS** Are there hand-washing facilities available at adult and tot level? Do caregivers and children use them regularly? Are diapers changed regularly?
- **DISCIPLINE** In what ways and for what behavior are children punished?
- **FACILITIES** Is the furniture and equipment in good condition?
- **NUMBER OF STAFF AND KIDS** Are there enough caregivers for the number of children present? Are the facilities overcrowded?

childproof your home

According to the U.S. Centers for Disease Control and Prevention (CDC), falls by children account for about 2 million emergency room visits each year in the United States. In Canada, 75 percent of all emergency room visits by children from birth to age 4 were a result of injuries that occurred around the home. Help prevent these and other household accidents, such as burns, choking, and electric shocks, with a few simple measures. If you crawl around the house at toddler level, you'll soon see what a child might encounter. The potentially hazardous areas listed in the box, right, are not exhaustive; for details of all the areas that should be childproofed, contact safety organizations such as the CDC or Health Canada (see page 169).

Make sure all child products you buy or receive as hand-me-downs meet current safety requirements. Product recall notices are detailed on the Web sites of the U.S. Consumer Product Safety Commission (www.cpsc.gov) and Health Canada (www.hc-sc.gc.ca). Read all instructions carefully before using a product to ensure that you do so correctly, and check for sharp edges, mechanisms that could trap fingers, or parts that may become detached and swallowed.

Fit child safety locks on cupboards and drawers storing glass, knives, medicines, or toxic cleaners.

✓ CHILDPROOF YOUR HOME

Keep your home an injury-free zone by doing the following:

☐ **Secure windows** Close and lock all windows within your toddler's reach or where he can climb up to them.

☐ **Clear stairs** Make sure stairs are well-lighted and clutter-free. Consider nonskid runners.

☐ **Create a safe kitchen** Keep sharp and hot objects well away from the edges of work surfaces. Fit guards to the range top.

☐ **Ensure electrical equipment is safe** Place cables out of a child's grasp and check that items can't topple. Cover unused electrical outlets with special plastic caps.

☐ **Make floors hazard-free** Don't over-wax hard floors, and clear up any spills right away. Secure loose corners on rugs, and ensure that wires and cables are tacked or taped down.

☐ **Make furniture secure** Check that any furniture that your children could climb on is stable and won't topple.

☐ **Regulate the water temperature** Set your hot water temperature to no more than 120°F (49°C) to prevent scalds.

☐ **Remove dangerous objects** Check that items that could be swallowed, such as coins and buttons, are out of your child's reach. Never let him play with plastic bags or wrappers.

☐ **Tie back hanging objects** Don't leave pull cords on curtains and window blinds dangling—they're tempting toys. Gather them out of harm's way with rubber bands.

☐ **Secure medicines** Keep all drugs, including vitamins, out of sight and out of reach. Choose products with child-resistant tops.

☐ **Check computer use** If your children use a computer, check that they are sitting correctly (see page 44) and that they take breaks every hour to rest their eyes.

detecting child abuse

Although many parents are fearful that strangers may attack their kids, the truth is that most abuse—emotional, physical, or sexual—is committed by close family members, family friends, or by people known to a child, such as teachers, ministers, or sports coaches. This can make abuse a very difficult problem to detect and resolve. Although each year there are about 2 million reports filed in the United States and 135,000 in Canada alleging abuse, experts believe that these are only the tip of the iceberg, and that many cases go unreported.

what constitutes abuse?

The legal definitions of abuse vary across different states, provinces, and countries. But most experts agree on general definitions. Neglect is the most common form of maltreatment. It occurs when parents or caregivers fail to provide children with sufficient food, clothing, shelter, protection, medical

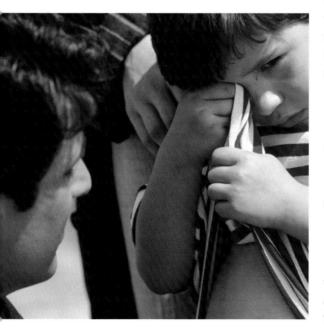

attention, or supervision. Emotional abuse is involved when parents or caregivers fail to give children love, approval, or acceptance. Also, children may be deprived of mental stimulation. Physical abuse is the deliberate infliction of injuries, pain, or excessive punishment on children. It might involve hitting, biting, kicking, beating, burning, or shaking. Finally, the rarest form of abuse is sexual. This is when children are forced to have sexual contact or take part in any sexual activity. It includes fondling, making a child touch an adult's sexual organs, and penetration, as well as indecent exposure and exposure to pornography.

what to do if a child reports abuse

It usually takes a lot of courage for a child to report suffering to an adult, so you have to be very careful about how you react. If a child merely hints that something has happened, encourage him to be open with you and provide assurances that you won't be angry. If a child is unwilling to talk, but implies that something is wrong, encourage him to talk to another family member or trusted adult. If the child is willing to talk, here's what you should do.

- **LISTEN CAREFULLY** Let the child explain in his own time. Try not to ask leading questions, such as, "Did he touch you?" Ask open questions, such as, "What did he do?"
- **STAY CALM** No matter what a child tells you, remain calm, be sympathetic, and assure the child that you believe him.
- **PRAISE THE CHILD** Explain that he did the right thing in telling you. Make sure that the child doesn't feel guilty about revealing a

Your reaction counts if a child reports abuse. Don't appear angry, shocked, or disbelieving. Assure the child that he did the right thing and that you can help.

"secret," and explain that what the abuser did was wrong. Some children may believe that the abuse was their fault or that they encouraged or deserved it.

- **BE REASSURING** Try to make the child feel safe with you, and tell him that you can get help and stop it from happening again. Explain that this will involve telling other people.

what to do if you suspect abuse

If you see any of the signs of abuse (see box, right), or if a child confides in you, contact a child protection or welfare agency, a dedicated charity, or a law enforcement office as soon as possible—they will advise you of the best course of action. Seek medical help if necessary.

Don't be unwilling to get involved for fear that you are wrong or that there may be reprisals—and don't put it off, thinking somebody else will report the abuse. Give your name and contact information because you will be able to help those investigating the case. If you find it impossible to give information to the authorities, report the abuse anonymously rather than not at all.

how do you prevent abuse?

Tell children that if anyone tries to touch private parts of their bodies or asks them to do things that make them feel funny, they should tell you right away, whoever it is.

You can help raise awareness of child abuse by contributing to or working with children's charities, prevention or treatment programs, or parenting courses. Get to know other children and parents in the area and work together to provide better care and supervision of children.

If you find that too often you are yelling at your kids, hitting them excessively, or are having trouble providing for their needs,

recognize that this could be termed abuse. Before you cause any more harm, seek help from your doctor, counselor, social worker, or a charity dedicated to preventing child abuse.

BE ALERT TO ABUSE

Often, children are simply not able to reach out and let people know they are being abused. The abuser may have threatened them; they may think that no one will believe them; or they may fear being taken away from their families. Look out for the following signs, which may indicate abuse.

☐ **Aggression** The child may get angry easily.

☐ **Excessive modesty** The child may be unwilling to undress or attempt to keep himself covered while undressing.

☐ **Fear of contact** An abused child may be withdrawn and appear to shy away from or have little trust in somebody he knows.

☐ **Inappropriate sexual behavior** He may act out of character for his age group and be flirtatious or have an unusual interest in or knowledge of sex.

☐ **Insecurity** The child may lack spontaneity and cling to trusted adults. He may be eager to please, attempt to be perfect, and overreact to criticism. He may exhibit self-depreciation and claim that he deserves bad luck.

☐ **Physical evidence** There may be unexplained scratches or bruises; injury to the genitalia; bloodstained, soiled, or ripped underwear; or even venereal disease.

☐ **Severe psychological disturbance** An abused child may exhibit symptoms such as bed wetting, head-banging, running away, truancy, eating disorders, self-mutilation, or attempting suicide.

raising streetwise kids

You won't always be able to control your children's environment. The older they get, the more they will be exposed to the world and its dangers. Help your kids cope with what life throws at them, whether it's having to confront strangers, steer clear of gangs, or saying "no" to drugs and alcohol.

teach stranger awareness

Every parent shudders at the thought of his child being snatched by a stranger. But, according to the U.S. Department of Justice, kidnappings by total strangers make up less than 0.5 percent of violent crimes reported against juveniles annually. It's a sad fact that in many cases of kidnapping, the person involved frequently is known to the child. Either way, kidnappings can happen anywhere. You can't be with your children all of the time, so help them protect themselves by teaching how to stay safe in public places and how to deal with suspicious behavior in adults.

keep a record

If the worst happens and your child goes missing, the police will need as much information as possible. The KlaasKids Foundation, established after the murder of 12-year-old Polly Hannah Klaas, suggests the following.

- Take up-to-date photos and, if possible, videos that clearly show your children's faces.

- Collect a DNA sample. To do this, rub a cotton bud on the inside of each child's cheek. Place it in a plastic zippered bag and seal. Put that bag in another plastic zippered bag and label it with your child's name and the date. Store in the freezer.

- Wait until your children have a cut and collect a blood sample using the same procedure as for the DNA sample.

Being with friends helps keep strangers away. Explain that kids can look after each other and that they should always get help if they see another child in danger.

start young

Children are quick to learn and most vulnerable when small, so start discussing stranger awareness at an early age. When you set guidelines, let your children know that these are necessary for their protection. In turn, listen to your children's fears and encourage them to ask questions. When you discuss avoiding strangers, emphasize that this includes women, people offering gifts, candy, or a lift, and people who smile and seem friendly. Teach your children to:

■ **COMMUNICATE WITH YOU** Explain why you need to know where they are going, whom they are with, and when they are going to be back. Make sure that they know to call you if their plans change.

■ **FIND HELP IF LOST** Tell them what they should do if they get separated from you. Police officers are always friends, but if your children are in a store, they can go to the cashier or a security guard also.

■ **MAKE A CALL** Teach them how to phone you, a relative, and the police, and make sure that they carry enough change. Or consider buying your children cell phones or pagers so that you can be in contact with them at all times. Compile lists of people whom your kids can phone if they can't get hold of you. Put these in their school bags.

■ **SAY "NO" IF NECESSARY** Let them know that they are allowed to say "no" to an adult if that person asks them to do something that feels wrong, such as taking their picture or touching private parts of their body.

practice escaping

Discuss various scenarios and use role-play to help your kids understand what they should do if someone approaches them. Give them a chance to think for themselves by asking how they would react. Praise them for good responses and fill in any gaps. Tell them to run away from anyone they are not sure about, such as a man who exposes his private parts or asks them into his house or car. If this happens, your children should find help from someone who can be trusted—such as a mom with kids, a teacher, or a police officer—or they should phone you or the police.

Explain what they should do if they are grabbed. Children's responses should basically be the same as an adult's (see page 72): They should attract attention; try not to be taken elsewhere; struggle as much as possible to get free; and run away to find help. Tell your children not to worry about dropping heavy bags or coats if it will make it easier for them to escape. Practice self-defense techniques (see Chapter 3) and make sure they know where to hit or kick an attacker.

be in the know

Get to know your children's friends and their parents and keep an up-to-date record of their addresses and phone numbers. Walk the routes that your children might walk between school, friends' houses, and play areas, and look out for potentially hazardous spots. Warn your kids about shortcuts they should avoid.

> **Check that there are no visible name tags on your children's clothing or bags. A child is more likely to trust somebody who appears to know his name.**

Also, contact your local law enforcement agency and find out about registered sex offenders in your area. Without frightening your kids, make sure that they know to avoid these people and the areas in which they live.

avoid gangs

According to the Do It Now Foundation, a U.S.-based organization dedicated to educating young people about drugs, health, and behavioral issues, there are an estimated 23,000 gangs with 665,000 members in the United States. In Canada, according to a Federation of Canadian Municipalities report, there are far fewer highly organized gangs, but there are many youth groups involved in increasing levels of violence. This has caused gangs to become a major concern to police and parents—both in inner-city areas and rural communities.

what constitutes a gang?

Organized gangs that might be involved in crime and violence are probably quite different from the groups of friends your children normally hang around with at school. Organized gangs usually consist of members from the same cultural and ethnic groups; claim a certain neighborhood as their exclusive domain; and— one of their most distinguishing features—often have a strict hierarchy within the group.

Gang identification is reinforced when members wear particular colors or styles of clothing or use specific language, hand signals, or a sign to mark their territory.

Parents who believe their kids are involved in gangs fear this also means their kids commit criminal activities. There are, however, different types of gangs. According to C. Ronald Huff, a professor in the Department of Criminology, Law, and Society at the University of California, there are three categories: hedonistic gangs, which aim to get high and commit few crimes; instrumental gangs, which perpetrate crimes against property and whose members use, but don't sell drugs; and predatory gangs, which commit violent crimes and deal in drugs.

why might my child join a gang?

Gang members come from all levels of society and ethnic backgrounds, and most join gangs for similar reasons:

- **EXCITEMENT** Kids who don't have out-of-school interests, perhaps due to lack of motivation or opportunities, find stimulation and variety in gang rituals and activities.

WHAT HAPPENS WHEN...

CHILDREN WATCH TV VIOLENCE

The American Academy of Child and Adolescent Psychiatry reports that just one violent TV program can increase aggressiveness in a child. Prevent your kids from becoming immune to violence by making sure that the programs and movies you allow them to watch aren't glorifying it or making it seem funny. Look instead for movies and programs that send positive messages about settling conflicts, learning skills, and achieving goals. If violence does appear, discuss the issues with your children.

- **PROTECTION** With a group of friends to back them up, kids can get a feeling of power and become more confident as their status rises.
- **WEALTH** If the gang takes part in theft or drug dealing, gang membership can lead to money. This is a particular motivation in inner-city areas where poverty is greater.
- **SOCIAL SUPPORT** Being with others who look and act the same gives kids a sense of camaraderie and belonging.

what are the effects?

The problems for children who join gangs are numerous. Many initiation ceremonies include beatings by other gang members to test courage and prove allegiance. As a member you must obey the rules, which can include committing crimes, sometimes against friends or family. Although not all gangs are involved in drugs, there is evidence that gang members are more likely to take them than other children and teens. Also, gang members may engage in underage sex.

Gang conflicts are particularly worrisome because they appear to be triggered by petty disagreements. Members of opposing gangs will kill over such minor infractions as making eye contact or showing disrespect. Some of this hypersensitivity may be attributed to drug-induced paranoia, or it can be a way of reinforcing the strict rules and hierarchy of the gang. Violence is also self-perpetuating, as the more violence a gang commits, the more its members are isolated from society and bonded to each other. Kids who are gang members may become immune to violence, and it comes to be a normal part of life. Once in a gang, it can be difficult to find the motivation or the courage to leave, as many ex-gang members have been beaten severely or even killed for disloyalty.

how you can help

There are two ways to deal with gangs: prevention and cure. Because children and teens often join gangs to gain respect and confidence, good parenting can go a long way toward preventing them from joining in the first place. Encouraging open dialogue with your children is always important. However, more specifically, it can be useful to find out about gangs in your area, where they are based, what they wear, and what they do. Discuss the subject with your children and explain why you don't want them to join a gang. Talk about the dangers of violence, drugs, and crime. Also discourage

RECOGNIZE GANG MEMBERSHIP

If your child shows some of these characteristics, he may have joined a gang:

☐ **Behaves oddly** He acts out of character and becomes more aggressive.

☐ **Comes home late** He stays out later than normal with no good reason.

☐ **Hangs with new friends** He abandons old friends and spends most of his time with different people.

☐ **His schoolwork suffers** He shows a lack of interest in school and may start to skip classes or drop grades.

☐ **Has more money** He suddenly spends more than usual on new clothes, gear, or activities.

☐ **Displays symbols** Names or pictures associated with a gang are drawn on books, clothes, or displayed in his bedroom.

☐ **Carries a weapon** He may start to carry a knife or even a gun.

them from wearing gang colors or hanging around with gang members, as they may begin to adopt their values.

A report by the U.S. organization Fight Crime: Invest in Kids, a nonprofit group that aims at preventing childhood crime, states that:

Most juvenile crime occurs in the hours between 3:00 and 6:00 P.M.

So encourage your kids to be constructive with their free time—particularly during these hours. Consider organizing a local youth group yourself with help from other parents or the

After-school clubs not only offer supervision but get kids involved in positive activities that give them a sense of belonging and self-confidence.

school. Make your children feel good about themselves with encouragement and praise, and set an example yourself by getting involved in the school and the community.

If you suspect that your child has become involved with a gang, contact your local police department or a school counselor for advice. Consider confronting your child. If you do, try to control any anger you may feel and ask to discuss it openly. Find out about his reasons for joining and in what sort of activities the gang is involved. Encourage your child to leave the gang with your help and the assistance of somebody he trusts, such as a sports coach, the police, a school counselor, or a minister. If you have knowledge of gang activity in your area, report what you know to the police, the school, and other parents.

combating drugs and alcohol

Unfortunately, teens—and sometimes children—think that drinking or taking drugs will make them look older and more sophisticated. Even a normally levelheaded teen can succumb to peer pressure or curiosity. As adults we know better, but how do we communicate this to kids?

educate yourself

You will probably be familiar with signs of drunkenness but may not know how drugs affect the mind and body. Here are some common drugs and their effects; for detailed information, look up a drug advice organization on the Internet (see page 169).

- **AMPHETAMINES** This drug is usually taken as a tablet. Short-term effects include: talkativeness, aggression, paranoia, reduced appetite, dilated pupils, and auditory and visual hallucinations. Amphetamines can be addictive and lead to aggression.

- **CANNABIS** There are two main forms of this drug: Marijuana consists of green, dried leaves and flowers; hashish is a compressed resin. Both are usually smoked in "joints" or pipes. In the short term, cannabis can produce a sense of well-being and relaxation, distort perception, affect coordination, and cause problems with memory. Cannabis use can increase the risk of cancer.

- **COCAINE** Sold as a crystalline powder, which is snorted or injected, or as chunks or rocks of "crack," which are smoked, cocaine raises alertness and increases energy levels. A cocaine user may have dilated pupils and insomnia also. Cocaine is physically addictive and can lead to paranoia. "Crack" use may lead to violence.

- **HEROIN** Sold as a white to brown powder or as a tar-like substance, heroin is injected,

According to the U.S.-based Office on Smoking and Health, most young people who smoke regularly continue to smoke in adulthood. They are also three times more likely to drink alcohol, eight times more likely to use marijuana, and 22 times more likely to use cocaine. Help your kids avoid smoking by encouraging them to be physically active and to take care of their health. If you smoke, acknowledge that it is bad for your health and a very tough habit to break. Try not to smoke in the home or only do so in certain rooms. Emphasize that resisting peer pressure is a sign of independence and strength.

smoked, or snorted. A user may experience euphoria followed by a period of drowsiness accompanied by slurred speech and constricted pupils. Heroin use can lead to serious health problems, such as collapsed veins, infection of the heart lining, and liver disease. Heroin is addictive and withdrawal symptoms—such as vomiting, pains and cold flushes—may appear within hours.

- **INHALANTS** Hundreds of household products can be sniffed or inhaled to get high, including lighter fluid, cleaning fluids, correction fluid, and hairspray. Signs are similar to drunkenness and include slurred speech, nausea, and loss of coordination. Inhalants can cause damage to the kidneys or liver. Sniffing high concentrations can cause heart failure or suffocation and death.

- **MDMA OR ECSTASY** This is usually sold as tablets, which may be imprinted with a logo. Associated with clubs and "raves," ecstasy can increase energy and enhance the senses. A user may experience tremors and tense muscles also. Ecstasy can lead to nerve cell damage and psychiatric problems. When on ecstasy, a user's increased body temperature can result in organ failure and death.

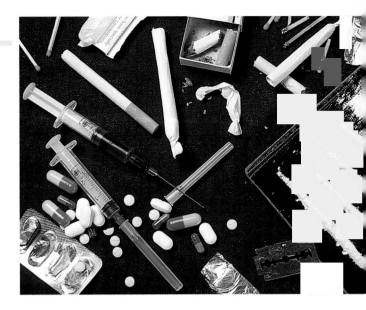

Physical evidence in your child's room or school bag might provide a clue. You might find empty bottles, lighters, rolling papers, syringes, razors, or even the drugs themselves.

KNOW THE SIGNS OF DRUGS

It can be difficult to tell whether changes in your child's behavior are due to hormones or to substances she's been taking. Here are some signs to look out for:

☐ **Severe mood changes** In one moment, your child may seem very happy, talkative, and full of energy, while in the next, she may become oversensitive, depressed, or withdrawn.

☐ **Tiredness** Your child may have less energy than usual and sleep at irregular hours.

☐ **Changes in appearance** Over time you may notice that she has lost weight and looks unhealthy, with pale skin, a runny nose, bloodshot eyes, or dark circles under the eyes.

☐ **Trouble at school** Your child may skip classes and start to drop grades.

☐ **Changes in lifestyle** She may start to stay out late, lose interest in her usual hobbies, and hang around with new friends.

☐ **Missing money** You might notice that money disappears from around the house or that pocket money gets spent very quickly.

☐ **Lack of concentration** Your teen might become a bit forgetful or start to lack coordination.

talk to your children

Don't wait until after the event—try to prevent drinking and drug taking by discussing it openly with your children. If you are worried that they won't listen to you, ask an older brother or sister or a friendly cousin to have a chat with them. Make sure that whoever talks to your children knows how to go about it. Sitting your children down for a lecture is not the best approach. Try these techniques:

- **PICK YOUR TIME** Don't discuss the problems of drugs and alcohol while your children are drunk, high, or hung over. Choose a moment when you can talk rationally and everyone is relaxed—perhaps while you're out for a walk or shopping. This should set the tone by making the subject more approachable.

- **LISTEN** This talk should not be a one-way conversation. If you don't give your children a chance to express opinions, you risk alienation. Ask what they know about alcohol and drugs. Do any friends use them? Have they ever tried them?

- **TAKE A STAND** Without being patronizing, express your views about drugs and alcohol. Say that you love your children and wouldn't like to see anything ruin their physical and mental health and that this is why you have rules about not using drugs or alcohol.

■ **POINT OUT THE CONSEQUENCES** Back up your argument with facts. Explain not only what alcohol and drugs can do to your health in the long term, but also the short-term dangers. Warn that not all people react in the same way to drugs and that nobody knows how he will react to a drug each time. Driving under the influence of drugs or alcohol is particularly dangerous. According to the National Crime Prevention Council, alcohol-related car crashes are the number one killer of teenagers in the United States.

■ **DISCUSS ALTERNATIVES** Think of positive activities that can help steer your children away from drinking and drugs in the first place. Many activities, such as clubs or sports teams, will be monitored and are an effective way of beating boredom.

provide support

There are lots of other things you can do to prevent your children from getting involved with drugs or alcohol. Take an interest in what they do in and out of school. Make sure you set a good example, drink moderately, and don't leave wines or liquor on display but lock them away. By keeping in touch with the school—both teachers and other parents—you will be able to exchange information about drug or alcohol abuse among local youngsters. You also can find out about specific drug education programs, such as Drug Abuse Resistance Education (DARE), which operates around the world and uses uniformed police officers to teach children how to resist peer pressure and avoid drugs throughout their school years.

Practice refusing drugs or alcohol with your kids. Point out that it takes confidence to refuse peer pressure, but that you believe your children have the strength to do it.

seek treatment

Many teens try drinking or drugs once or twice—it's a part of growing up, so don't overreact if you find that your children have done so. Talk about it and work through some of the strategies previously mentioned. However, if you think that your children are regular drinkers or drug takers, they may already be psychologically or physically addicted. If this is the case, seek professional help from your doctor, a school counselor, or the police, who can put you in touch with local treatment centers. Try not to panic; you will have to work together with your children to help them stop. Be encouraged that many people have fully recovered from addictions.

be safe at school

According to a report published in 2000 by the Josephson Institute of Ethics based in California, more than one in three teens in the United States report not feeling safe at school. Incidents such as the Columbine shootings and stories of theft, violence, drugs, and bullying focus attention on how difficult it is for parents or guardians to protect their children when away from home. However, there are things you can teach your children that can help ensure their safety during school hours and when traveling to and from school.

know your school

Although your children are probably safer in school than anywhere else, you will feel more confident if you are familiar with the buildings and the routines. Ask your children if they feel safe at school. Are there regular fire drills? Does the school discuss bullying, drug-taking, and

check security

Visit your child's school and get the answers to the following questions:

- Does the school have any preventive measures in place, such as ID cards for students and staff, spot checks with metal detectors or dogs trained to sniff out drugs?

- Do staff members know how to identify troubled students, and are counselors on hand to help them?

- Are all staff members informed about the school's strategies for dealing with drugs, gangs, weapons, and general security?

- Have the police checked out the safety of the school, and does the school have a designated law enforcement officer to educate the children and act as a contact for help?

- Is there a conflict resolution program in place?

- Are there crisis preparedness guidelines in place?

Have a secret password that your children can ask of whoever comes to pick them up. If your children are unsure, tell them to find a teacher and phone you.

other antisocial activities? Have your children ever had anything stolen? Do any children bring weapons to school? Is it easy for a stranger to get into the school grounds? Talk to them about gang behavior and drug-taking that happens on or near the school premises (see pages 138 and 141), and encourage them to report such problems to teachers. Explain that doing so isn't being disloyal to friends but is helping to create a better school environment.

You could also visit the school to find out about security measures yourself (see opposite). Arrange to discuss the issues with those in charge, or raise them at a parents' meeting. If there are any shortfalls, get involved in fixing them. Speak to other parents, along with the school staff and the school board, about introducing safety strategies and supporting the school. This will set a good example for your children about how best to resolve problems.

travel with caution

As with all regular journeys, you and your children should not get complacent about the trip to and from school. If you teach your children how to look confident and be on guard from an early age, they should continue this caution into later life.

driving to school

Driving your kids to school will ensure that they are accompanied from the moment they leave the house until they reach the school gates. If you're carpooling with other parents in your area, your children should know exactly who is driving them each day. Be sure they understand that they shouldn't get into a car with somebody they don't know, even if the driver tells them that it is his turn that day. Explain that he might be trying to trick them.

Bike helmets should be adjusted to sit on the top of the head, not tilted back at an angle, and the straps should always be fastened.

If you or the designated driver is going to be late, notify the school to satisfy yourself that your children will be cared for until you turn up. Don't send someone in your place without warning your child or the staff.

walking or cycling

If your children walk or ride their bikes to school, remind them that there's safety in numbers. Ideally, an adult should accompany them, but if this isn't possible, make sure that they walk or cycle with one or more of their friends. The U.S. Centers for Disease Control and Prevention recommends that children ride on sidewalks or paths until they are at least 10 years old. Older children can ride on the road once they have good riding skills and can observe basic rules, such as using hand signals, maneuvering through junctions, and obeying traffic signs. Consider walking the route so that you can point out any busy junctions or blind spots where they should get off their bikes and use pedestrian crossings. It is vital that they wear bright, reflective clothing and helmets that fit snugly and all round the head. Check that their bicycles are well maintained with good brakes, a headlight, and a rear reflector.

using the school bus

If your children's school operates buses that meet local safety regulations, this is probably one of the safest ways for kids to get to school. Vulnerable periods include waiting for the bus and when getting on and off. Make sure your children know that they should leave enough time to catch the bus. If they have to wait around, they should try to stick with their friends at the bus stop. Explain that the driver can't see all around the outside of the bus, so they should never cross the road behind it and should be at least 10 ft. (3.5 m) in front and wait for a signal from the driver before crossing. Stress the importance of good behavior on the bus. They should: Keep the aisles clear; not distract the driver; and stay in their seats until the bus has come to a stop and it's time to get off. If any other children bother them on the bus, they should report it to a bus monitor, if available, or to a teacher at school.

taking public transportation

Children should take the same precautions as adults on public transportation (see page 52), but there are a few extra considerations. Children aged 12 and under should always be accompanied to and from school by a responsible adult or older child; if they can travel in a group, so much the better. Remind your children to stay alert and look confident wherever they go. When choosing a seat on a train or subway, tell them never to sit in a car alone but to stay near others, preferably

families. If everyone gets off, they should move to another car as soon as possible. On a public bus, your children should stay near the driver.

Tell your children that if they are threatened on public transportation—it doesn't matter whether it's an adult getting too close or other kids trying to steal from them—they should make a fuss and seek help as soon as possible. If there is an emergency call button, they should press it, and seek help from a police officer, uniformed staff, or an adult with other children.

stay safe on school trips

Visits to firehouses, farms, museums, or sports games are all common extracurricular activities, but away from the school, how can you be sure that your children are receiving adequate care and supervision? And what can you teach your children about staying safe? One answer is to get involved and volunteer to act as a supervisor. However, we don't all have time to do this, so here are a few other ideas.

contact your school

The chances of an accident happening on a school trip are very low; student safety is paramount to the teachers, administrators, and the site being visited. If you have any concerns, raise them with your child's teachers. Ask for the full names and contact details of at least two teachers on the trip—in case you need to contact them in an emergency. Also, find out about:

- **LOCATION** Where exactly are the students going and, if appropriate, what is the address of their accommodation?
- **NUMBER OF STAFF AND KIDS** What is the chaperone-to-student ratio?
- **EMERGENCY PROVISIONS** Will there be a first aid kit on hand? Will all the teachers or supervisors carry cell phones or radios?

- **PROCEDURES** Is there a roll call at regular intervals? Are students expected to stay in pairs or groups if they are unaccompanied? And are the meeting points and times given out to each student and explained clearly?

provide medical information

Make sure that the school and the teachers on the trip have your contact details in case of an emergency, and notify them in writing if your children suffer from any allergies or medical conditions, such as asthma, epilepsy, or diabetes. If your children need regular or emergency medication, such as an inhaler, a shot of adrenaline (Epi-Pen), or insulin, make sure that the accompanying teachers have these and have been trained in how to administer them.

discuss the trip

Take an interest in the trip, and encourage your children to get the most out of it. Instill a feeling of responsibility in them by stressing how one person's behavior can affect everyone's safety and enjoyment. Stress that there is an educational purpose to the trip and that they should not get too excited or lose concentration. Also, remind them of all the normal precautions regarding crossing roads, telling chaperones their whereabouts, and not talking to strangers. If they are going abroad, remind your children to respect the local culture and customs.

Investigate the activities the children will be taking part in and make sure that safety equipment is provided and the instructors are fully qualified to teach children.

dealing with bullying

An article published in the *Journal of the American Medical Association* in 2001 reported that 8 percent of children in the United States said that they were being bullied on a weekly basis. The effects of bullying can be devastating, made worse by the fact that many children keep the problem secret—feeling powerless to stop the perpetrator. For parents, it is terrible to think that their child is being victimized.

Whenever children are suffering at the hands of bullies, they must be supported and any incidents treated seriously. The longer a problem goes unresolved, the more chance of physical and psychological damage. In some cases, bullying has even led to suicide. In order to protect your children, it helps to understand what they might be experiencing.

what is bullying?

Bullying takes many forms. In some cases, a child may not even realize that he is being bullied. Bullying can appear to start at random—for example, if one child decides that another is annoying—but it also can be more specific, perhaps because a friendship has broken down. Some bullying may be racially motivated, and this can often be detected by the language used. Other bullying may be sexual and may include molestation. Whatever the basis, bullies use:

- **EMOTIONAL MANIPULATION** A bully may ignore what the victim says, laugh at his mistakes, steal his bag, or exclude him from a group.

Walking away while looking alert and confident is the best defense against bullies. Tell him not to fight back unless necessary, but rather to firmly say "Leave me alone."

- **VERBAL ABUSE** A bully may persistently tease, call names, make nasty comments, and spread rumors about the victim.
- **PHYSICAL ABUSE** A bully may inflict bodily harm upon his victim, including causing bruises, making cuts, or pulling hair.

what makes a bully?

Children and teens who bully seem to do it because they want to feel powerful and more liked than their victims. Studies have shown that many have grown up in environments in which physical punishment is acceptable, and that they have learned to settle arguments with their fists. In most instances, bullies disguise their actions and find excuses for arguing with their victims. However, some bullies can become so confident that they don't care who sees what they are doing. This kind of behavior usually emerges when nobody does anything to stop it.

what you can do to help

Initially, you should provide good opportunities to talk to your children about their day at school. If one of your children tells you of an incident—no matter how minor—stay calm and be positive.

Reassure your child that he was right to tell you about bullying and, most important, let him know that the incident was not his fault.

Inform the school immediately. Ask the teachers or a school counselor for advice, and request that an official record of the incident be made. Many schools have bullying intervention programs in place, but if there aren't any at your children's school, contact administrators and discuss the introduction of techniques such as class discussions or peer counseling.

If the bullying continues, and you're not happy with the school's response, make official, written complaints, first to the principal and then the school board. It will help if you have a record with dates of all incidents. If the bullying persists, or if your child is physically or sexually assaulted, you can report it to the police.

LOOK FOR SIGNS OF BULLYING

Children are sometimes reluctant to admit to being bullied. If you suspect there is something wrong, watch for signs such as these:

☐ **Refusal to go to school** A child may pretend to be ill in an attempt to miss school and be reluctant to go when forced.

☐ **Poor grades** A child does less well on tests and homework and concentrates less in class.

☐ **Social isolation** A child may fall out with previously good friends who won't necessarily be the bullies but may be unwilling to associate with a victim.

☐ **Distress** Things that wouldn't normally upset a child may suddenly become more important and cause frustration, tears, or aggression.

☐ **Depression and low self-esteem** A normally happy child may become less motivated and lack confidence. He might avoid leaving the house. When questioned about this behavior, he may refuse to talk about the problem.

☐ **Damaged clothes and possessions** Bags, lunchboxes, and lunch money may disappear, and a child may come home regularly with torn or missing clothing.

☐ **Injuries** A child may suffer more bruises and cuts, which might occur on a regular basis.

away at college

New surroundings, new friends, and greater freedom mean there can be an awful lot for your teen to adjust to when going to college, and security and health concerns are probably the last thing on his mind. So, without appearing to interfere, check out the safety of your teen's campus and be prepared to offer advice. If your teen plans to travel while away at school, take a look at the tips on page 152.

Studying with others is much safer than studying alone. Tell your teen to leave a study area if everyone else does, and suggest he considers studying with friends.

keep your teen safe

Living away from home can be exciting for your teen, but worrisome for you. Take some time to talk about personal security. Stress that your child should trust his instincts; get away from threatening situations; seek help; and defend himself, if necessary.

Friends will play a big part in your teen's security at college. Remind your teen that there's safety in numbers, and encourage him not to leave a group at a party, bar, or club, and to stay together when going home late at night. With close friends, he can create a kind of "buddy system," in which the students provide

STREETSMART

CUT HEALTH RISKS The freedom at college can go to your teen's head and make him do or try things he wouldn't normally. Respect his maturity and have a calm and open discussion about the dangers of having unprotected sex and the risks of alcohol and drugs (see page 141).

each other with a copy of their schedules and tell each other of their whereabouts and expected return times. Ask your teen to give you the phone numbers of his close friends.

Many colleges arrange self-defense courses for both men and women; encourage your teen to contact campus security or the university police department for enrollment details.

Discuss safety on the streets. Remind your teen about the need to walk confidently and be aware of his surroundings, particularly if he has consumed any alcohol. Check that he knows how to determine safe routes both day and night, avoiding deserted or poorly-lighted areas. If he is being followed, he should head for a more populated area or go into a shop or café to get help. Many universities have escort services that shuttle students home on buses or walk them home late at night.

If your teen is going to be driving, talk about ways of keeping safe (see page 48), such as being alert when approaching the car; having keys ready in his hand; keeping doors locked and windows shut when driving; leaving space to maneuver in traffic; locking the car at gas stations; and parking in well-populated and well-lighted areas.

visit the campus and halls

If you are dropping your teen off at school, check out security measures together. Campus housing should be secure, with proper door and window locks and entry systems. Off campus,

your teen should consider installing window locks and other security devices in his apartment (see page 40). Help him check out the safety of routes between buildings and to look for the nearest fire escapes or security staff.

All colleges have campus security or police departments where students can go for help, and these should provide leaflets and/or Web sites giving advice. Check college security reports to see what types of crimes have been committed on campus; the more information your teen is armed with, the better he can protect himself.

PROTECT PROPERTY

Theft makes up a large proportion of the crime that takes place in residence halls or in campus classrooms. Encourage your teen to keep property safe with the following tips:

☐ **Carry appropriate ID** Student cards or other approved ID should be carried at all times and never loaned to others.

☐ **Don't leave notes on doors** Why alert thieves to the fact that no one is in the room?

☐ **Guard valuables** Small items such as cash, credit cards, and jewelry should be kept out of sight or locked up. Larger items, such as a computer, should be security marked (see page 38), tethered and locked to a desk, and never left in a room over vacation.

☐ **Lock up** Bedroom doors and first-floor windows should be kept locked.

☐ **Report strangers** People who act suspiciously or who don't wear required ID should be reported to security. Don't hold open doors for people who don't have a key or ID.

Bicycles are a target, so encourage your teen to lock his securely to bike racks or railings. Bikes also can be registered and marked by the police or engraved with a driver's license number.

trotting the globe

Independent travel is an excellent way to see the world on a limited budget. If your teen is planning a trip, he will probably want to arrange everything himself or with friends. However, if you do some of your own research, you'll be able to ask your teen some good questions and better prepare his for a trip. See also the travel advice on page 56.

plan carefully

Research the area well before your teen sets off; reputable guidebooks are a good place to start. The U.S. State Department and, in Canada, the Department of Foreign Affairs and International Trade provide up-to-date information on most

prepare for safe travel

Before your teen goes away, assure yourself of his safety with a few final checks:

■ Make sure he has travel insurance and that it covers luggage, medical bills, emergency flights, and any activities or sports in which he might take part.

■ Buy him an international phone card, which allows calls without the need for change. Many cell phones can be used abroad, but reception is limited in some areas—check with the phone company for details.

■ Ask your teen to give you an itinerary and a route plan. If possible, get the addresses of hostels or guesthouses where he will be staying. Remind him to tell you if any addresses, routes, or dates change.

■ Photocopy your teen's passport, tickets, credit cards, insurance details, and emergency phone numbers. Keep a set and give him copies to take with him.

■ Check that he is carrying a list of his health details, including blood type, allergies, medical conditions, and special requirements.

countries in the form of fact sheets or on Web sites, generally including details of any terrorist activities, crime, and road conditions.

Ask your teen to learn about differences in culture that might affect the way he interacts with locals, such as gestures, clothes, and eating and drinking habits.

Remind your teen that travelers are subject to the laws of the countries they are visiting. He should not overstay his visa or work illegally, as this could lead to a fine, imprisonment, or deportation. Stress that most countries have strict laws against drugs—some even impose the death penalty. For this reason, your teen should never carry anything for others and avoid associating with people who may be involved in drugs. If he gets into any form of trouble— including being robbed, attacked, or arrested, or if he becomes ill or gets injured—the local U.S. or Canadian embassy should be able to provide help and advice. The addresses of embassies can be found in most good guidebooks.

keep a check on health

At least six weeks in advance of the trip, make sure that your teen has found out which inoculations or special health precautions are needed for the countries he is visiting. Check also that he knows how to recognize the signs and symptoms of possible health problems. The Centers for Disease Control and Prevention (see page 169) provides country-by-country advice.

Take time to discuss the risks of alcohol consumption. In hot climates not only can it lead to severe dehydration, but it is also a factor in many holiday accidents: Drunkenness is often behind such incidents as people diving into shallow swimming pools or falling off balconies.

Arrange regular communication by phone or e-mail. If you decide that calls will be on a particular day, stress how worried you will be if that call is late.

be wary of strangers

When traveling, your teen is likely to meet lots of new people. Remind him to be wary of offers that seem too good to be true and of fellow travelers with "helpful" advice. Tell him not to accept food or drink from strangers unless it obviously comes from a reliable source. He should never bring strangers back to his room. Also, your teen should avoid hitchhiking—it's never safe, wherever you are in the world.

Although many people travel alone with no problem, a young traveler will be much safer with others. If your teen cannot persuade a friend to go along with him, he could consider traveling with an organized group. There are now several travel companies that specialize in trips for single travelers.

secure rooms and protect possessions

If your teen is off on a long trip, it's likely that he is going to be staying in fairly cheap accommodations. Encourage him to choose the safest rooms possible, with intact, lockable windows and solid, lockable doors. No matter how short of money your teen is, he should never sleep on beaches or in stations.

For added safety in rooms, on the street, or when traveling on buses or trains, your teen might consider some of these travel items:

- **BACKPACK LOCK** Some that allow you to secure a pack to something solid may include a wire mesh that covers the pack to prevent knife slashes. Other locks secure zippers only.
- **DOOR LOCK** Padlocks or bicycle-style chain locks can be used to reinforce weak locks.
- **DOOR WEDGE** Doors can be strengthened quickly with a standard door wedge. Wedges with built-in alarms are also available.
- **MONEY POUCH** Whether worn around the neck, chest, waist, or leg, these pouches should be concealed beneath clothing.
- **SMOKE DETECTOR** Small, portable smoke alarms can give peace of mind in countries where detectors are not required in rooms.
- **TRAVEL ALARM** Many alarms can be attached to doors or windows or placed in luggage so they sound if disturbed. Some have a pin that can be pulled in case of personal attack.

Purchase these items at your local travel store or on the Internet (see page 170).

6

safety for older people

Living alone and health problems can make older people feel more at risk of becoming a crime or accident victim. Discover ways that you can combat specific concerns, such as home security, trips and falls, con games, and elder abuse.

feel safe in and out of the home

Many people worry that as they get older they will become less able to defend themselves and their property from theft and attack. Figures from the U.S. Bureau of Justice Statistics show, however, that in the United States in recent years people over the age of 65 experienced less violence and fewer property crimes than younger people. The risks are greater, though, that older people will be targeted for telemarketing tricks or "get-rich-quick" schemes. The following tips show how older people can safeguard homes and avoid such con games, so that they do not feel so vulnerable at home.

make a home secure

Most crimes against older people occur in or near the home. But home security can be improved by using certain devices, practicing caution with strangers, and getting support from the community. For more tips on home security see page 40. Also, the crime prevention officer at your local police department may be available to view the premises and give advice on any extra security measures needed.

be wary of strangers

Many thieves gain entry to older people's homes by pretending to be salespersons, repair people, charity collectors, or survey compilers. Many seniors accept lines such as: "We're checking for a gas leak"; or "There's a problem with your phone line and we need to check it." Instead, they should use their peephole and ask for photo ID so that the person's name and company can be read. Then they should contact the company

Many alarm systems connect to the police or a security company when activated so that help will arrive immediately. A lot offer bedroom panic buttons, too.

▌STREETSMART

KEY SAFETY Never leave house keys underneath a potted plant, doormat, or in a mailbox. Also, don't leave spare car keys in your vehicle. Instead, leave any spare sets of keys with a trustworthy neighbor.

to make sure the call is legitimate. If it is, the employee will understand the delay. Seniors should arrange for repair or delivery people to arrive at a specified time and should never let a stranger know if they are in the house alone.

Older people should also be wary of anybody who keeps them talking at their door or in the yard; he may be distracting them while an accomplice breaks into the house.

If a stranger asks to make a telephone call from the house, an older person should ask the stranger to wait outside while she makes the call, even in an emergency.

If a stranger won't leave, the homeowner should call the police immediately. If the stranger is already in the house, however, he shouldn't be prevented from leaving—personal safety is paramount. Go to a neighbor's house and call the police from there instead.

Finally, nuisance calls from telemarketers (see page 158) can be screened using the answering machine. Friends and family should be told to speak up on the machine so that their calls will be picked up when recognized.

be part of the community

One of the main reasons that thieves target older people is that they are more likely to be isolated, perhaps because they live alone, don't have many visitors, or can't get to the phone easily. So older people should encourage friends or family members to visit each day, and get to know their neighbors so that they can look out for each other. They should get involved in a neighborhood watch program or crime prevention support group aimed at seniors—the local police department should be able to supply information on programs in the area.

For the greatest peace of mind, consider investing in a house alarm system. If an entire system is not practical, there are a number of low-cost devices that do a good job of reinforcing various parts of the home. Here are some of them:

☐ **Door reinforcers** These are U-shaped pieces of metal that fit around the lock edge of a door to make it more resistant to kick-in attacks.

☐ **Metal plates** These can be attached on both sides of a door in order to reinforce the area around the dead-bolt lock.

☐ **Door frame reinforcers** One of these fits down the hinge side of the door frame, and another is attached down the lock side, to make your frame stronger, and your house safer.

☐ **Anti-lifting device** Fit one of these to patio doors—a key target for burglars—to prevent the opening door being lifted and removed.

☐ **Window shock sensors** These devices attach to windows, and detect vibrations associated with breakage or tampering.

☐ **Garage door locks** Garages can present an easy way for burglars to gain access so fit strong locks to the bottom corners of the vehicle access door. Consult a locksmith if you are unsure which type to choose.

☐ **Vent locks** These are attached to windows to stop them being opened past a certain point.

☐ **Garden shed locks** Use padlocks to protect your garden shed if you store anything of value there, and make sure both they and the door hinges are tightly secured.

☐ **Motion detector lights** These will light up if movement is sensed, so they can deter prowlers, or warn you of their presence.

☐ **Alarms** There are many types of alarms; some monitor doors and windows and others detect sound or movement within a room. For further details, see page 40.

avoid scams

Older people are a favorite target of scam artists because seniors are often trusting and unaware. As a result, fraud victims may be robbed of their life savings and any sense of security they had. Unfortunately, incidents often go unreported because the victims are very embarrassed or feel that it is their fault. Con artists are experts in persuasion and may make many attempts before they achieve success. To be better protected, older people should be aware of the schemes.

know the tricks of the trade

Con artists will try to contact older people in many different ways—by phone, knocking on

the door, or by mail. No matter which approach they use, at the root of all schemes will be an attempt to persuade older people to give, spend, or "invest" money for little or no return. Deals that sound too good to be true usually are. Here are some scams to watch out for:

- **CONTRACTS** Insurance policies, sales agreements, or any type of contract should never be signed without being read thoroughly. Also, numbers for credit cards, bank accounts, Social Security, or Social Insurance should never be given to a stranger on the phone, whoever he claims to be.
- **PRIZES AND SPECIAL OFFERS** The news of winning a fabulous prize should be greeted with suspicion, especially if money needs to be sent to cover minor expenses. Similarly, watch out for prizes offered to entice people to buy a product or service—there should be no purchase necessary to win. Some con artists even send a courier to pick up money, which is never seen again. And the prize is then worth less than the money lost.
- **CHARITY DONATIONS** Whether they phone, arrive on your doorstep, or put an envelope in your letterbox, groups that ask for a donation should be thoroughly researched first. Ask to be sent a financial report; reputable charities will always be happy and willing to send one when asked.
- **INVESTMENTS** "Get-rich-quick" schemes always have a catch. A pyramid scheme is a classic example. In this, somebody will ask for an investment of money—perhaps in a small company—for which the investor is guaranteed a good return. Others are

Check all contracts thoroughly; a review by a professional or trusted friend or relative is a good idea so you are clear about the contents of the agreement.

encouraged to invest, and with each person persuaded comes a share of that investment. However, such schemes collapse when people fail to find enough investors or when the con man suddenly gets caught.

- **CREDITS AND LOANS** Credit or loans might be offered by some companies in return for a "small" upfront fee. But don't give up any money—legitimate companies won't ask for payment in advance.

- **CREDIT CARD NUMBERS** Somebody pretending to be from a bank, credit card company, or law enforcement agency might call or visit and say that he needs help tracking down a criminal. Then he'll ask for bank account details, a credit card number, Social Security, or Social Insurance number. If that person were really investigating a crime, he would have access to that information.

- **WORK FROM HOME** Many newspapers, posters, and leaflets advertise jobs that people can do at home to earn money quickly. But to get started, they need to buy supplies or take a course first. If they send in money, they are unlikely to get much in return—at least anything that will help them earn a living.

- **HEALTH PRODUCTS** "Miracle" products to prevent baldness, help lose weight, or build muscles may entice some people, but many of these don't work, and they may even be damaging to a person's health.

- **REPAIR PEOPLE** Somebody who turns up on the doorstep or calls on the phone might offer home or car repairs. Some might offer to do a simple job at a very cheap price, but then "discover" a much bigger problem that needs to be fixed and will cost a lot more. When looking for a repair person, seek advice from friends and family and always try to deal with a well-established firm. Don't pay

Trust word-of-mouth rather than advertisements to find a skilled, reliable, and good-value repair person. Ask friends and family for a recommendation.

for any work until it has been satisfactorily completed. If paying by cash, always be sure to get a receipt.

- **SALES PEOPLE** A sales person can be quite aggressive in getting people to agree to a deal or sign a contract. Be suspicious if a salesperson requires an immediate signature—a legitimate company will give people time to check the details. Try shopping around for other quotes before agreeing to anything, and always compare the exact terms and conditions of the deal.

report any incident

Con artists manage to catch intelligent people of all walks of life, so older family members should not be embarrassed if they think that they may have been victimized. Don't try to get the money back by using a company that claims to be able to recover lost funds—it may be just another trick. Report the incident to the police, the local consumer protection office, or a consumer protection group. This may help catch the criminals and prevent future scams.

SENIORS NEED TO GET UP FROM A FALL

In case of a fall, an older person should first check how badly he is hurt. If it's serious, or the person feels he can't get up unaided, he should call out for help. If alone, he should try to get to a phone, or use a panic button—some are voice-activated, allowing a person to call via a pendant around the neck. If it's not serious, he should take his time to slide or crawl to the nearest chair or table for support. He should then remain seated until he recovers her composure.

prevent accidents

To keep themselves safe, older people need to take care with their medications, and look out for potential hazards that could cause a fall.

follow a pill routine

Seniors should make sure their family knows their pill-taking routine. All their prescriptions should be filled at the same pharmacy so that a record can be kept, and they can be advised of any possible drug interactions. A personal record should be kept of medications and doses, too, and a copy put in an emergency supply kit if they have one (see page 20). Weekly pill holders can help keep track of each day's dose.

prevent falls

According to the support group Seniors Safety (www.seniorssafety.com), slips and falls are the main cause of injury and death among those

over 65, but there are many ways to minimize the chances of an accident. Regular exercise, like gardening, gentle walking, or swimming for half an hour a day, is enough to improve strength, balance, and coordination. Also, eyesight should be checked annually, and prescription glasses renewed if necessary. When given a prescription, older people should check that the medication won't cause dizziness. They also should check for areas in the home that need to be fall-proofed (see opposite).

get a medical alert

Older people who live alone should sign up for the services of a medical response provider (see page 170). These organizations come to people's aid when members phone or activate a panic button. They will also notify friends or family if an accident occurs. Medical warning items, such as a bracelet, locket, or key ring provide vital medical information or ID if a person is unconscious or unable to speak. People with allergies or conditions that might require emergency medical treatment, such as diabetes, epilepsy, or asthma, should keep emergency medications in the house and/or on themselves.

All medication should be taken in a well-lighted room so that the instructions can be clearly read. Ask a pharmacist to explain any directions that are unclear.

fall-proof a home

According to the Canadian-based support group Seniors Safety (see opposite), 60 percent of falls occur in the home, so check potential trip and slip hazards like those described below.

Other tips are to wear low-heeled shoes with non-slip treads; install handrails and place non-slip mats in the shower and bathtub; install strong, easy-to-hold handrails on both sides of all stairways, and always keep the stairs free of clutter.

1 CARPETS Check that all edges are secure and that there are no worn patches. Avoid using small scatter rugs; otherwise use only rugs with non-slip backing. You can make rugs slip-proof by attaching double-sided, adhesive carpet tape.

2 CORDS Keep telephone cords or electrical cables at the edges of the room, and secure them with cable clips or tape.

3 LOW FURNITURE Position low tables, footrests, and other low items near the edges of the room, clear of major pathways.

4 CHAIRS When possible, sit in high, hard chairs rather than low couches. Always get up slowly from a sitting or lying position.

5 STORAGE Don't put items that are used often on high shelves. If you do need to reach something, use a grabber, or stand on a secure stepladder with rails.

6 LIGHTS Make sure both the outside and inside of the house are well illuminated, particularly in the halls, on stairs, and in the kitchen and bathrooms. Change dead light bulbs straight away.

Keep flashlights handy in case of a blackout. Nightlights aren't just for children; they'll light the way from the bedroom to the bathroom, too.

7 PANIC BUTTONS Many household alarm systems offer buttons connected to a monitoring station. Install these near to the ground so they'll be accessible in case of a fall. Wear portable panic buttons during the day and keep them by the bed at night.

8 FLOORS Clean up spills on smooth surfaces straight away. Don't wax wooden or tile floors.

prevent elder abuse

Every year, hundreds of thousands of older people in the United States and Canada are the victims of some form of abuse. According to the U.S. Administration on Aging, 90 percent of known perpetrators of abuse and neglect were family members; other perpetrators were long-term caregivers. Here are some tips on how to recognize elder abuse and what to do to stop it.

what constitutes abuse?

Elder abuse is generally divided into four main categories, each of which has different signs:

- **PHYSICAL ABUSE** This is the infliction of pain or injury. Along with hitting, pushing, shaking, burning, or kicking, this also includes sexual abuse, the inappropriate use of drugs, or force-feeding. Injuries may be visible on the victim. And they may feel unable to offer explanations for injuries or may try to make excuses.

- **NEGLECT** This happens when the caregiver fails to provide adequate food, shelter, clothing, hygiene, medical treatment, or other basic needs to an older person. Symptoms can include malnourishment, dehydration, hazardous or unsafe living conditions, inadequate clothing, bedsores, lice, a smell of urine or feces, overmedication, sedation, or untreated health problems.

- **PSYCHOLOGICAL ABUSE** This is the infliction of emotional or mental anguish and includes insults, harassment, humiliation, intimidation, or threats. Other types of emotional abuse include isolation or treating an older person like a child. A victim of this may appear upset, agitated, depressed, withdrawn, or noncommunicative. The victim may avoid eye contact, be evasive, or show signs of dementia, such as rocking or sucking.

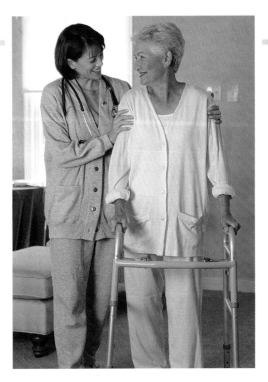

Choose home care carefully. Make sure the agency is accredited and that individual carers' training, references, and criminal records have been checked.

- **FINANCIAL EXPLOITATION** This happens when somebody illegally or improperly uses an older person's funds or assets, usually for his own benefit. It can include theft of money and possessions, forgery, improperly cashing checks, and coercion or deception, perhaps to get an older person to sign a contract or will. Signs of this might be unusual withdrawals or transfers of money; sudden change of wills; bills and rent unpaid without explanation; and poor clothing and housing when the older person can afford better.

what to do if abuse is suspected

An older person may be reluctant to report abuse, particularly if it is being committed by a family member. She may be embarrassed that it is happening, or too scared to mention it. If you know anyone who is showing any of the above symptoms or has told you that she is being abused, seek help. Be wary of accusing anyone directly, as this may make the situation worse. If you can speak to the older person in private, you should try to persuade her to report the abuse. If you can't do this, report what you suspect to social services, adult protective services, state abuse hotlines or, in the case of nursing homes in the United States, to the local long-term care ombudsman, details of whom you can find on the Web site of the National Citizens' Coalition for Nursing Home Reform (www.nccnhr.org). If there is immediate danger to the victim, however, simply call the police.

stay safe outside

Attacks on the street happen to people of all ages, but older people often feel more vulnerable, as they can't easily run away or fight off an attacker. However, there are simple precautions they can take to avoid an attack. Being suspicious of people may not be in everyone's nature, but being too carefree can make people an easy target for a criminal.

protect possessions

Older people should protect themselves on the streets in the same way as anyone else (see Chapter 2). But according to the U.S. Bureau of Justice Statistics, there is an annual average of 46,000 purse and wallet snatchings from people over 65. To avoid becoming victims, seniors should use money belts, fanny packs, or concealed pockets to carry small valuables only. Those who carry a bag always should keep it closed, and shouldn't carry it with the strap across their body—they could be hurt if someone tries to steal it. Also, carry a personal attack alarm—both to attract attention and to scare an attacker away. Older people should use the self-defense techniques in Chapter 3, which are simple and require little strength.

take care with money

Older people should not keep too much cash in their homes or in the bags that they carry around; pensions or other regular payments should be sent directly to their bank account. Money should be counted as quickly as possible when in shops or banks. It is important to be aware of who is nearby, and to alert the staff if anyone is acting suspiciously. Particular care is needed when using automatic teller machines (see page 32), and if seniors have any trouble using a machine, they should contact their bank—not ask a stranger for help. They should not carry their personal identification number with their cash cards and should never tell anyone the number, even bank employees. See page 30 for further advice on maintaining the security of credit and charge cards.

pay particular attention

Certain belongings tend to be main targets for thieves, so older people should take extra care with these items when outside the home:

- Never carry large amounts of cash. When paying for things, try not to pull out wads of money at a time; bring out only the money needed. Carry a $20 bill in a separate pocket to give to a mugger if threatened. Also, keep some small change in a pocket to call a relative or cab in case of an emergency.

- Try not to wear a lot of jewelry when going out alone, especially expensive-looking items. And cover up jewelry when in public places.

- Keep cell phones in a pocket or bag—don't carry them by hand. Use them when in a shop or building.

- Carry home keys separate from the rest, when possible. This way, if a key ring gets stolen or is lost, you can still get into your home.

resources

Reporting crime can help the police change a high-crime neighborhood. But what can you do personally to make your community a safer place? Understand what happens when you go to the police and learn the benefits of neighborhood watch programs. Also, find out phone numbers and Web sites of helpful organizations.

crime watch

Dealing with crime and accidents can be a daunting process. You may be reluctant to get involved or unsure of what you should do. This section looks at what happens when you contact emergency services. And if you join a neighborhood watch program, you may help prevent crime from happening in the first place.

reporting crime and accidents

A call to 911 should be used to contact the police, an ambulance, or the fire department if a crime is under way or if somebody's life is in danger. For example, 911 would be appropriate

KNOW HOW TO CALL 911

When you call emergency services such as 911, tell the dispatcher whether you need the police, fire department, or an ambulance. Then, listen to the dispatcher's questions and answer them as best you can. You will need to give the following information:

☐ **Where you are calling from** Give this number in case you are cut off or if the dispatcher needs to call you back.

☐ **What the emergency is** Describe what has happened. If somebody is injured, say whether he is conscious and breathing.

☐ **Where it is** Give the address, if known, or the name of a nearby bar or shop, the road you are on and direction you are traveling, or distance from the nearest town.

☐ **Who needs help** Tell the dispatcher how many people are involved and their ages.

☐ **Who you are** Give your name.

in the case of serious traffic accidents, fires, or the presence of an intruder, but isn't designed for reporting petty theft (see below).

If you are in an emergency situation, your first priority should be to get to a safe place with a phone or a place where you can use your cell phone to call 911. Stay on the line if it takes a while for someone to answer—you will be dealt with. Provide detailed information about the emergency (see box, left). If there is a medical emergency, the dispatcher may provide first aid instructions, such as how to perform cardiopulmonary resuscitation (CPR). Don't hang up until the dispatcher tells you to do so.

non-emergency situations

To report a crime such as a theft from a vehicle or criminal damage, call your local police station rather than 911. This will keep the 911 service available for those in immediate danger.

Be patient if you are waiting for the police to respond to a nonemergency crime. There is no need to call repeatedly—this can slow down the process. Depending on the situation, the police may send an officer to your home, take a report over the phone, or you may be asked to report the incident in person at the police station.

visiting a police station

When you arrive at a police station, you will see a receptionist. He will listen to you and take your report or he may introduce you to another officer, who takes you to a quiet room, so you can speak in confidence.

You will be asked questions and will be encouraged to give as much detail as possible. The officer will want to know, for example, where and when the incident occurred; what exactly happened; whether there were witnesses; and a full description of the attacker, including any small details you noticed, such as nervous habits, the language used, accent, or smells.

Don't be embarrassed if you think you did the wrong thing during the crime, and be completely honest. The police are not there to judge you, and it might look bad if it emerges later that you lied or exaggerated anything in your report. When you have given your report, you will be given a crime report number and the name of the officer who will be investigating your case. You should keep this information for reference and for your insurance, if relevant. The police will also be able to give you advice

DNA IS SAMPLED

Deoxyribonucleic acid (DNA) is a chemical structure found in the cell nucleus of plants and animals. The reason it is vital in fighting crime is that patterns within DNA are virtually unique to everyone, and so cell samples can be taken from crime scenes or from a victim and then matched to a sample from a suspect. This is why, when reporting an attack to the police, you should: not wash; stay in the same clothes or put the relevant clothing in a plastic bag; keep any evidence of an attacker, such as half-eaten food or a tissue; and tell the police if you scratched the attacker with your nails or a key. If the crime was in your home, don't clean up until the police say you can. Thanks to DNA matching, cases of rape and murder from long ago can sometimes be solved, and people who were found guilty of a crime can sometimes be proved innocent.

on support groups. If you have experienced a personal attack, the officer will advise that you have a physical examination.

What happens next depends on whether the police catch anyone and whether they then have enough evidence to arrest the suspect. They may contact you with further questions and ask you to attend an identity parade or appear in court, although attendance in court is not mandatory. However, it may happen that the police don't catch anyone or can't take the case to court for lack of evidence. Prepare for this in your mind, and don't let it discourage you from reporting an attack in the first place. The more the police are told about crime in the area, the better they will be able to develop strategies to deal with it. There may be repeat offenders or a pattern may develop. This sort of information will ultimately help the police to protect you and others.

DNA testing involves scientifically comparing samples of blood, semen, skin cells, or hair from crime scenes with similar samples from a suspect.

neighborhood watch programs

First started more than 30 years ago, neighborhood watch programs have been an invaluable asset in helping the police fight crime. Also known as Block Watch, Town Watch, and Crime Watch, these programs encourage neighbors to be the extra eyes and ears of a community. The emphasis is on reporting crime—not tackling criminals yourself.

getting started

If your area does not already have one, the best way to set up a neighborhood watch program is to contact your local police or sheriff's department, which will provide you with relevant information. There are excellent Web sites that offer advice—contact the crime prevention organizations on the opposite page.

You'll need to start off with a meeting to gauge the level of local interest. Publicize it with fliers, posters, and door-to-door visits. At the meeting you should explain to everyone

how a neighborhood watch program works and stress that it is not for vigilantes, but involves reporting suspicious activities to the police. If there is sufficient interest, you can hold more meetings to elect a chairperson and block captains, who coordinate the activities. You will need to establish ways of communicating with each other, such as with leaflets, a newsletter, or a Web site.

making the most of your program

Activities will vary according to the level of commitment and the level of crime in the area. Residents should be encouraged to look out for one another, listen for unusual sounds, such as breaking glass, and look out for suspicious activities, such as a stranger talking to children. Your local law enforcement agency can help train people in observation techniques. In addition, you might consider:

- **HOUSE WATCHING** If a resident is away, organize people to keep an eye on his house.
- **FACT GATHERING** Check police reports on crime in the area and share the information locally.
- **HOME SECURITY TRAINING** Ask a local law enforcement officer to give a talk on improving security in the home.
- **HOME VISITS** Get to know older people in the area and discuss checking on them.
- **PROPERTY MARKING MEETINGS** Arrange for people to bring items to be engraved or marked with an indelible pen (see page 38).
- **CITIZEN PATROLS** Coordinate a group to patrol the area by car or on foot. No weapons should be carried, and a law enforcement officer should train volunteers.

Get together a group to clean off graffiti or to spruce up your local park; it will help build community spirit and make your area a more pleasant place in which to live.

useful organizations

IN THE UNITED STATES

general

Centers for Disease Control and Prevention
www.cdc.gov
800-311-3435

Federal Bureau of Investigation
www.fbi.gov
202-324-3000

Federal Trade Commission
www.ftc.gov
877–FTC–HELP (877-382–4357)

National Safety Council
www.nsc.org
630–285–1121
800–621–7619

National Security Institute
nsi.org
08–533–9099

National Sheriff's Association
www.sheriffs.org
703–836–7827
800-424-7827

Salvation Army
www.SalvationArmy.org
800–SAL–ARMY (800-725-2769)

U.S. Department of Justice
www.usdoj.gov

auto safety

American Automobile Association
www.aaa.com

The Center for Auto Safety
www.autosafety.org
202–328–7700

National Highway Traffic Safety Administration
www.nhtsa.dot.gov
888–DASH–2–DOT (888-327-4236)

child safety

American Association of Poison Control Centers
www.aapcc.org
800–222–1222 (for emergencies)

Child Care Aware
www.childcareaware.org
800–424–2246

Childhelp USA
www.childhelpusa.org
800-4–A–CHILD (800-422 4453)

Connect for Kids
www.connectforkids.org

KlaasKids Foundation for Children
www.klaaskids.org
415–331–6867

National Center for Missing and Exploited Children
www.ncmec.org
800–THE–LOST (800-843–5678)

National Childcare Information Center
nccic.org

The National Clearinghouse on Child Abuse and Neglect
www.calib.com/nccanch/

Partnership for a Drug-Free America
www.drugfreeamerica.org
212–922–1560

Prevent Child Abuse America
www.preventchildabuse.org
800–CHILDREN (800-244-5373)

Security on Campus
www.campussafety.org
888–251–7959

crime prevention

Equifax
www.equifax.com
800–685–1111

The Metropolitan Burglar and Fire Alarm Association of New York
www.mbfaa.com
718–894–6712

National Citizens' Crime Prevention Campaign
www.weprevent.org
800–WE–PREVENT (800-937-7383)

National Crime Prevention Council
www.ncpc.org
or www.mcgruff.org (for kids)
202–466–6272

Neighborhood Watch
www.usaonwatch.org

resources

emergency planning

American Red Cross
www.redcross.org
877–272–7337

Federal Emergency Management Agency
www.fema.gov
800–480–2520

food safety

Food Safety and Inspection Service
www.fsis.usda.gov
202–720–7943
800-535-4555

gun safety

Brady Center to Prevent Gun Violence
www.bradycenter.org

Internet safety

The CERT Coordination Center
www.cert.org
412–268–7090

International Web Police
www.web-police.org
317–823–0377

WiredPatrol
www.wiredpatrol.org

older people's safety

AARP Foundation
www.aarp.org
800–424–3410

MedicAlert Foundation
www.medicalert.org
888–633–4298

National Center on Elder Abuse (NCEA)
202–898–2586

Plainsense
www.plainsense.com

overseas travel

The Bureau of Consular Affairs
travel.state.gov
202–647–9576

Federal Aviation Administration
www.faa.gov
800–255–1111

Outpac Designs Inc. (for Pacsafe)
www.pac-safe.com
800–873–9415

Overseas Security Advisory Council
www.ds-osac.org
202–663–0533
800–499–8696

Summit Hut
www.summithut.com
800–499–8696

Walkabout Travel Gear
www.walkabouttravelgear.com
800–852–7085

personal attack

The Antistalking Web Site
www.antistalking.com

Arming Women Against Rape and Endangerment
www.aware.org
877-672-9273

Criminals Behind Bars
www.criminalsbehindbars.com

The Help Line USA
561–615–4029

The National Center for Victims of Crime
www.ncvc.org
800-FYI-CALL (800-394-2255)

National Domestic Violence Hot Line
800-799-SAFE (800-799-7233)

The Rape, Abuse and Incest National Network (RAINN)
www.rainn.org
800–656–HOPE (800-656-4673)

Rape Crisis Centers
www.rapecrisiscenter.org
800–870–5905 (English)
800–223–5001 (Spanish)

Survivors of Stalking
www.soshelp.org

work safety

National Institute for Occupational Safety and Health (NIOSH)
www.cdc.gov/niosh
800–35–NIOSH (800-356-4674)

Occupational Safety and Health Administration (OSHA)
www.osha.gov
800–321–OSHA (800-321-6742)

U.S. Equal Employment Opportunity Commission
www.eeoc.gov
202–663–4900
800-669-4000

IN CANADA

general	**Canadian Legal FAQs** www.law-faqs.org
	Canada Safety Council www.safety-council.org 613–739–1535
	Department of Justice Canada canada.justice.gc.ca 613–957–4222
	Government of Canada canada.gc.ca 800-O-CANADA (800-622-6232)
	Health Canada Online www.hc-sc.gc.ca 613–957–2991
	Royal Canadian Mounted Police www.rcmp-gc.ca
	Salvation Army www.salvationarmy.ca 416–425–2111
auto safety	**Transport Canada** www.tc.gc.ca 613–990–2309
child safety	**Block Parent Program of Canada** blockparent.ca
	Canadian Centre for Abuse Awareness www.abuserecovery.net
	Canadian Centre on Substance Abuse www.ccsa.ca 613–235–4048
	Canadian Safe Schools Network www.cssn.org 905–848–0440
	Child Find www.childfind.ca 204–339–5584
	Stay Alert Stay Safe www.sass.ca
crime prevention	**Canada's Business and Consumer Site** strategis.ic.gc.ca 800–328–6189
	National Crime Prevention Centre www.crime-prevention.org

	National Capital Region: 613-941-9306 Elsewhere: 877–302–6272
emergency planning	**Canadian Red Cross** www.redcross.ca 613–740–1900
	Office of Critical Infrastructure Protection and Emergency Preparedness www.ocipep.gc.ca 800–830–3118
food safety	**Canadian Food Inspection Agency** www.inspection.gc.ca 800–442–2342
gun safety	**Canadian Firearms Centre** www.cfc-ccaf.gc.ca 800–731–4000
Internet safety	**WiredPatrol** www.wiredpatrol.org/international/canada
older people's safety	**Canadian MedicAlert Foundation** www.medicalert.ca 800–668–1507
	The National Advisory Council on Aging (Health Canada) www.hc-sc.gc.ca/seniors-aines 613–952–7606
overseas travel	**Department of Foreign Affairs and International Trade** www.passages.gc.ca 800–267–6788
personal attack	**Access to Justice Network** www.acjnet.org
	Canadian Association of Sexual Assault Centres www.casac.ca 604–876–2622
	Education Wife Assault www.womanabuseprevention.com 416–968–3422
	World Wide Legal Information Association www.wwlia.org/ca-stalk
work safety	**The Canadian Centre for Occupational Health and Safety** www.ccohs.ca 800–263–8466
	Canadian Human Rights Commission www.chrc-ccdp.ca 888–214–1090

index

acknowledgments

I would like to take this opportunity to thank certain people for all of their support and encouragement. This includes my family, especially my parents, for always instilling in me the belief that anything is possible in life. [Mom and Dad, I hope this proves you right.] Also, big thanks to my sister, Debi, for her fantastic skills on the computer keyboard. And thanks to my housemate, Lorna, for keeping me going when I was tired after working full time during the day and then on my book until late into the night. I wouldn't have eaten properly for months if it hadn't been for her meals. Thanks go also to: my true friend, Vanessa, for introducing me to my publishers and making my dream come true; Mick, my self-defense partner and best friend; The Metropolitan Police for endorsing the book; and all my friends and colleagues who have wished me well and kept me going to the end. Special thanks go to my publishers for having the courage to do this book and for all the hard work they have put into it. Great teamwork; thank you all so much—I had a blast.

Carroll & Brown would also like to thank:

Additional editorial assistance Dr. Louise Aikman, Annie Bridges, Tom Broder, Fiona Screen, and Kelly Thompson

Production Director Karol Davies

Production Controller Nigel Reed

Computer Management Paul Stradling

Picture Researcher Sandra Assersohn

Indexer Hilary Bird

Models Brett Alexander, Anna Amari-Parker, Frank Cawley, Mark Curnock, Emma Deacon, Sylvia Firth-Tuck, Justin Ford, Tristan Hickey, Louise Lang, Charlotte Medlicott, and Dorothy Wong

Hair and Makeup Jeseama Owen

picture credits

Page 7 Craig Blankenhorn/Fox, **8** Powerstock, **11** Nicolas Russell/Getty Images, **12** Powerstock, **18** and **19** Jules Selmes, **23** Denise Hager/Bubbles, **26** Juan Silva/Getty Images, **27** Abbie Enock/Travel Ink, **28–29** Powerstock, **30** Alan Danaher/Getty Images, **32, 34, 42, 47** and **48** Powerstock, **50** and **51** Auto Express, **52** Powerstock, **53** Sally & Richard Greenhill Photo Library, **54** Simon Bottomley/Getty Images, **56–57** Daniel O'Leary/Panos Pictures, **58** Frank Herholdt/Getty Images, **60** Stephen Swintek/Getty Images, **61** G & M David de Lossy/Getty Images, **115** David Drebin/Getty Images, **118** Studio MPM/Getty Images, **122** G & M David de Lossy/Getty Images, **125** Jim Varney/Science Photo Library, **127** Powerstock, **129** Michael Kelley/Getty Images, **130** Getty Images, **131** Adrian Green/Getty Images, **133** Jules Selmes, **134** Bruce Ayres/Getty Images, **136** Getty Images, **138** Powerstock, **142** R Nicholas/Art Directors & TRIP, **144** Marc Romanelli/Getty Images, **145** Jules Selmes, **147** Education Photos, **150** G & M David de Lossy/Getty Images, **151** Bill Ross/Corbis, **153** Paul Smith/Panos Pictures, **155** Erik Dreyer/Getty Images, **156** Ron Chapple/Getty Images, **158** Loisjoy Thurstun/Bubbles, **159** Christopher Bissell/Getty Images, **160** Ken Huang/Getty Images, **162** Ariel Skelley/Corbis, **167** Dr Jurgen Scriba/Science Photo Library, **168** Powerstock

Cover and **117**, Bertram Henry/Getty Images